Monitoring, Measuring, and Managing Customer Service

Monitoring, Measuring, and Managing Customer Service

Dr. Gary S. Goodman

Jossey-Bass Publishers
San Francisco

Jossey-Bass books and products are available through most bookstores. To contact Jossey-Bass directly, call (888) 378-2537, fax to (800) 605-2665, or visit our website at www.josseybass.com.

Substantial discounts on bulk quantities of Jossey-Bass books are available to corporations, professional associations, and other organizations. For details and discount information, contact the pecial sales department at Jossey-Bass.

Library of Congress Cataloging-in-Publication Data

Goodman, Gary, S.
  Monitoring, measuring and managing customer service / Gary S. Goodman.
    p. cm.
  ISBN 0-7879-5139-0 (alk. paper)
    1. Customer services—Quality control—Handbooks, manuals, etc. 2. Customer services—Evaluation—Handbooks, manuals, etc. 3. Customer services—Management—Handbooks, manuals, etc. I. Title.

HF5415.5 .G67 2000
658.8'12—dc21   00-025368

FIRST EDITION
HB Printing   10 9 8 7 6 5 4 3 2 1

The Jossey-Bass Business & Management Series

DEDICATION

This book is dedicated to my wife, best friend, and colleague, Dr. Deanne Goodman, and to our wonderful daughter, Amanda Leigh Goodman, of whom we are so proud.

CONTENTS

ACKNOWLEDGMENTS

I would like to thank my editor at Jossey-Bass, Cedric Crocker, for his support during the writing of this book. I am also grateful to Cheryl Greenway for her efforts in coordinating the project. I'd also like to thank Stacey Sawyer for her help with copyediting the manuscript.

And I'm grateful to you, the working customer service professional. Without your ideas and help, this book wouldn't be possible.

Dr. Gary Goodman is an internationally recognized innovator in customer service, sales, and telemarketing. He consults on a national basis for a number of Fortune 500 companies, including Xerox, Polaroid, and Kraft General Foods. He is also a best-selling author of twelve books, and his seminars are offered by numerous universities across the country, including UCLA.

Dr. Goodman earned his B.A. and M.A. degrees at California State University, Northridge; his Ph.D. at the Annenberg School for Communication at the University of Southern California; his Juris Doctorate at Loyola Law School, Los Angeles; and his Advanced Executive M.B.A. at the Peter F. Drucker School, Claremont Graduate University. His articles are featured in numerous business publications, and he is a frequent expert guest on scores of radio and television programs, worldwide. He is also a dynamic keynote speaker at corporate meetings and at conventions and trade and professional associations.

Before becoming a full-time speaker and consultant, he was a former professor at DePauw University; the University of Southern California; and California State University, Northridge. Currently, he is president of The Goodman Organization, based in Glendale, California.

Monitoring, Measuring, and Managing Customer Service

Introduction

Excellence in customer service doesn't come about accidentally. It needs to be carefully defined, planned, and managed. What you'll find in the following pages is a true system for creating and sustaining excellent customer service.

Is this book right for you?

This book is for you if you manage or supervise people who have the words customer service, customer care, customer support, client services, or client relations in their job title.

This book is for you if you are a senior manager of operations or a general manager. If so, you'll find many of its policies, procedures, and quality controls new and useful.

Or, you could be in charge of or supervise technical support or run a credit and collections division; in this book you'll find information that applies to your work and to those you manage.

You could be a vice president or a senior vice president of sales or marketing who wants to learn how to transform customer service into a profit center. Here you'll find new and practical ideas for making that transition feasible.

You could be a director of human relations who will find many of this book's new ideas about recruiting, retaining, and compensating service personnel worth exploring.

You could be responsible for training or monitoring service people; if so, you'll find the new measurements and communication tools exceedingly helpful. Finally, you might want to generate a corporate commitment to achieving first-class customer service; this book will discuss how you can make that happen.

This book does not include the fluff that comes with typical books or seminars. I won't waste your time, incessantly lecturing you about the value of customers. You already know how important they are. However, I will show you, with an unprecedented level of detail, how to communicate with customers and how to win their loyalty.

My consulting clients have helped me to refine what I am going to share with you in these pages. They invested substantial resources to create true service breakthroughs. They also took career risks in supporting what we hoped would work but had to go out on a limb to prove.

On a personal level, I owe my consulting clients a tremendous debt of gratitude. They enabled me to do what I have been schooled to do: apply original thinking to improve people's lives.

So, get ready for a different kind of customer service book. I promise you that its methods, while new and sometimes counter-intuitive, actually work. As I've said to numerous clients, "Try them; you'll like them!" But I must warn you, if you wait to like them before you try them, you'll delay increasing your appreciation of how first class customer service is created and sustained.

Best,

Gary

How to Consistently Produce Great Customer Service

Tomorrow is customer appreciation day!

This is the inscription on the U.S. Postal Service's building in Glendale, California, that I see as I pull into the parking lot to check my mail box. The thought occurs to me that I won't be coming to the post office tomorrow, so I'll miss the festivities. What are the postal workers going to do to show their appreciation?

I have to pick up a parcel at the front desk, so I figure I'll ask one of the friendly clerks what tomorrow has in store. But by the time I reach the front of the line, I'm bushed. I have time only to say: "I'm going to miss Customer Appreciation Day tomorrow, so, would it be too much to ask if you could appreciate me, today, instead?"

In all seriousness, it's unusual that an organization, public or private, would single out a specific day to show its gratitude, especially in this heralded era of the customer. I would have thought that, in each nook and cranny, American outfits would uniformly display framed mission statements that proclaim that the customer is always number one. Of course, the trick isn't announcing that we deliver excellent service—it is actually delivering it, day in and day out, across all the transactions that we have with those who support us. But how can we achieve consistently great service? You'll learn the answer to this question as you read this book. Most of us have had at least one great customer service experience that we can quickly summon to mind. For example, I purchased a dozen white business shirts from the local Nordstrom department store several years ago. Mysteriously, the cotton in them shrank so much that I couldn't get into them. Because I was busy traveling for my consulting practice, I didn't bring the problem to the attention of anyone at my local store for several months. Then, one day when I was shopping at Nordstrom's, I casually mentioned that I was disappointed with the shirts. Without hesitating, my Nordstrom salesperson invited me to return them. I'll never forget our brief conversation.

"Well, I have a dozen of them," I replied. "And I did get some use out of them," I added, wanting to be fair.

"Doesn't matter," he said. "Please see me when you come back."

And I did. I counted out the shirts on the elegant counter. He measured me for new shirts and promised to deliver them to my home. Sure enough, a dozen crisp replacements were handed to me at my door that very evening—completely free-of-charge!

This is an example of great customer service. I have a very strong hunch that you'd agree that Nordstrom went out of its way to speedily and comfortably solve my problem.

There are a number of ingredients that are common to most great service events. In this chapter, I'm going to identify what they are and then provide you with a formula for making what seems to be exceptional service an everyday experience for your customers. This chapter will set the stage for the rest of the book, where you will learn special methods for coaching, counseling, monitoring, measuring, and managing your people.

ELEMENTS OF GREAT SERVICE

We could go on all day defining great service though the use of inspirational stories such as the one about Nordstrom. However, mere examples of fine service won't enable us to accurately identify or replicate the components that are common to these situations. We don't want to place ourselves in the awkward position of Supreme Court Justice Potter Stewart, who found he was at a loss for words when defining a legal phenomenon. All he could do was blurt out: "Well, I know it when I see it!"

We don't have to settle for a non-definition of great customer service. We will examine the topic more closely and identify the core **behaviors** that excellent service personnel provide. Moreover, we'll look at the **results** that excellent service produces, as well as the reliable means for **producing** and **measuring** these results as they occur in everyday customer contacts.

But first, let's turn to the ten basic characteristics of superior customer service.

1. Vendors seem eager to solve our problems. They don't go into hiding in the stockroom when they see us carrying one of their bags back into the store. They don't duck our phone calls or make us "cool our heels" before responding to our letters, faxes, or e-mails. In a very real sense, they seem to have a positive attitude irrespective of whether their merchandise is marching out of, or heading back into, their stores.

2. The reason they are so calm is that they take a long-term view of customer relationships. They don't have a temporary tent operation where they sell fireworks between the 2nd and the 4th of July, after which they disappear before the sparklers fizzle out. Generally, vendors who provide great service recognize the simple fact that there is a tomorrow. They appreciate that creating goodwill is going to produce repeat business and a long stream of future income from happy customers.

3. They don't blame customers for contributing to their own mishaps. The Nordstrom salesperson could have blamed my dry cleaner for shrinking my shirts to doll-size. Or, he could have asked me if I had gained a little weight since buying them. That could explain the impression I had that they were smaller in all the wrong places. In other words, there are many excuses that the Nordstrom associate could have used to weasel out of helping me. Happily, he didn't try to use any of them.

4. They try to do at least one extra thing that customers don't expect but nonetheless appreciate. The sales rep took it upon himself to deliver my shirts to my home, saving me the hassle of waiting while he assembled and packaged them.

5. They value our time, knowing it has a cash value as well as a recreational value. Heck, we could be doing any number of things besides returning an item. They appreciate that their mistake is a grinch who is gobbling up our precious hours.

6. They honor any expected ceremonial expectations that customers may bring to transactions. I have a V.I.P. card at a local restaurant where I'm a regular. This card entitles those at my table to a free appetizer. When I make reservations, I mention that I'm a V.I.P. diner, and, as a general rule, the reservationist notes this fact. Therefore, when I come in, the host places a small V.I.P. card on my table, signaling the waiter to bring the appetizer without being asked.

This pleasant gesture says, "You're special, and this is one way that we're going to communicate this to you and to everybody else." But what happens when this process breaks down—no card is placed on the table, and no appetizer magically appears?

I have to ask for both; then the appetizer will be served. But some of the sheen of the dining experience has been rubbed off by the lapse, and my enjoyment diminishes, ever so slightly. Otherwise, the service may be first-rate, but it won't reach the highest level of excellence that I had expected.

The moral of the story is this: If you raise customer expectations, make sure that you deliver what is expected. Otherwise, you'll create an expectation/performance gap, which sows the seeds of dissatisfaction.

7. They always apply the essentials of service. Even if our vendors don't have special V.I.P. classifications for us, we still need to feel that we're being treated with respect and that our business is appreciated. So, when we enter a business, in person or via the telephone, we should be greeted in an upbeat way that tells us we are truly welcome. As we leave, we should also be thanked for our business.

For instance, Antonio, who opened a good restaurant about ten years ago, always remembered that we were some of his original patrons, and he always made it a point to show his gratitude. Even if he had been speaking to other customers, he'd interrupt himself, leap to his feet, and thank us for coming in as we were about to depart. He made it his business to quietly monitor how our meal was progressing, while always placing himself close by so he could wish us a good evening.

This ritual of appreciation is an excellent habit to adopt. I've noticed that Antonio has now trained all his hosts to do as he does.

8. They provide performance or satisfaction guarantees. Another element of great service is the provision of an implicit or an explicit guarantee. Indeed, customers increasingly expect to receive guarantees from those with whom they do business. In many cases, the availability of a guarantee will determine whether a prospect will choose to do business with us or someone else.

Here are several situations in which it is essential to offer a guarantee:

a. **When you're the new kid on the block.** In this case, a guarantee might do you a lot of good. Let's say you're just starting out and having to fight entrenched competitors. How do you get people to give your product or service a try? Try offering a money-back guarantee to take the financial risk out of it. Hampton Inns took the lead in this area a few years ago by offering a refund for the first night's stay if the lodger found it unsatisfactory. This was a way to garner major attention for a new national chain while asserting a quality pledge that differentiated it from its many competitors.

b. **When there has been negative publicity or harmful word-of-mouth information about your product, you might need a guarantee.** It will serve to reassure people who are interested in buying from you but who are leery of your reputation.

    The Jaguar automobile is an example. I've never met anyone who isn't impressed with the looks of most Jaguar automobiles. But, not too long ago, the WALL STREET JOURNAL reported that many owners' Jaguars had mechanical problems. As a result, Jaguar responded by offering the public a 30-day free test drive.

    Other car companies, such as Audi, went further by providing full-maintenance contracts with their new cars. These promotions don't seem to last long. They're short-term expedients, but they can restore a sense of confidence.

c. **When your product or service is a true innovation you'll probably need a guarantee.** One of my clients is the fellow who sold part of the Berlin Wall, one tiny piece at a time. Remember those little rocks glued onto plaques that were sold in department stores? His idea. He sold a million plaques in six months. They came with certificates of authenticity—frameable guarantees.

d. **You'll want to offer a guarantee when your product or service aims to change the public's buying habits.** The client who sold the Berlin Wall came to me with a new product. It purifies water one drop at a time, through a handheld, pen-like dispenser. He asked for my opinion and I told him it would be marketable only with an unconditional guarantee, because folks weren't used to buying pure water that way. They're used to bottles and filters.

FedEx used a guarantee to get its overnight package delivery service off the ground. Could you sell Christmas trees or baby's first shoes or caskets by phone or through mail order? Probably not without strong guarantees, because you're changing important buying rituals and altering sentimental traditions.

e. **You'll generally need a guarantee when you're selling by phone or mail, especially when promoting sensory products that appeal to a prospect's taste, touch, or vision.** Fine art and vintage wines come to mind. A guarantee might assure a potential customer that the product will satisfy him or her without first having to try it.

f. **Winning back lost customers often requires a guarantee.** Why should unhappy customers risk disappointment or failure with you again? For this reason, bankrupt airlines, attempting to return to normal service, will offer satisfaction guarantees.

g. **When the risk of loss is high, or a product's potential defects are not subject to inspection, you should provide a guarantee.** Costly or technical items call for guarantees. That's why most cars, houses and computers are sold with warranties.

h. **Whenever your profit margins are relatively high, consider offering a guarantee.** Your additional sales will usually more than compensate for your losses from returns. The guarantee serves to attract marginal buyers, who might continue to sit on the sidelines unless they are shown that there is no risk involved in trying out your product or service.

Please note this important caveat: Your offer of a guarantee must be backed up by customer service representatives who will be pleasant when processing product returns and refunds.

One of my clients is in a studio photography business that offered a "complete satisfaction-or-your-money-back" guarantee, but they were obviously peeved when customers exercised it. They would interrogate customers before issuing the requested refunds.

I urged this company either to make the guarantee easy to invoke or to stop offering it. Raising service expectations by offering guarantees is perfectly fine providing we're also gladly willing to live up to them.

Guarantees are usually worth offering because they generate additional sales. They help customers to overcome their natural resistance to trying new items or items in which they don't have 100% confidence.

Guarantees also have an interesting effect on how we do business. When we strongly support a quality guarantee, we thus must build a product or service that meets or exceeds buyer expectations. This situation introduces a quality-oriented frame of mind in your firm and in your people. When a lot is expected of us, it's difficult to let our customers down.

9. Great service should be embedded into a behavioral routine, so it can be properly monitored, measured, and managed. We can all provide superior service, time and again, providing we have fully defined what it is and we have trained our people to deliver it.

Some companies make the mistake of trying to hire "great people" as a short-cut to providing great service. It doesn't work. As Peter F. Drucker has pointed out, there are very few great people, and, under the best of circumstances, they are distributed somewhat evenly across companies. No single company has a mo-nopoly on attracting them. That's why we need effective managers to bring great performances out of a *wide range of people* who may possess merely average social talents.

The same principle applies to hiring so-called "nice" people to perform in customer-service roles. From a behavioral perspective, there is no such thing as a nice person. There are, however, people who have learned to behave "nicely." Fortunately, everyone can be trained to perform service functions in a nice manner. We just need to define what "nice" means to customers.

For example, it's considered nice when customers are greeted by someone who smiles and who uses an ascending tone as she says "Hello!" or "Welcome to the Marriott!" Managers can measure "nice-ness" when it is defined and expressed behaviorally. They can recognize a smile and a rising voice, and these events can even be videotaped and reviewed to assure that they've occurred.

But if nice-ness isn't operationally defined, then it exists only as an *unsubstantiated inference* or as a *subjective judgment* on the part of the manager. This doesn't cut the mustard when it comes to appraising job performance. I wouldn't want my career to hinge on whether my manager guesses that I'm acting "nicely" or be based on a mere inference that I'm doing a good job.

Employees deserve explicit criteria to which they can make their behavior conform. This way, they can qualify for the highest raises and for the best promotions. In other words, great service shouldn't be personality-driven. It should be process-driven.

Accordingly, great customer service representatives (CSRs) shouldn't be regarded as a rare collection of super-nice or super-special people who possess unusual gifts for communicating with customers. They shouldn't be mythologized or be placed on a pedestal. Everyone in an organization should be challenged to deliver top-notch service—not just an "elite" group of gurus.

Great service providers should simply be perceived as exceedingly well-trained and well-managed people who can be counted on to duplicate a well thought-out and highly productive service routine.

Later in this chapter, I'll provide you with the specifics of a great service routine that you can implement over the telephone.

10. Customers emerge from service encounters with the perception that they've been treated exceptionally well. Ultimately, the most important function of customer service is to motivate customers to prefer our company and to express this preference through repeated purchases. Repeat business is probably the best path to achieving rising revenues with lower sales costs.

A great service encounter will contribute mightily to producing customer loyalty. It will arouse in the customer the perception that he has received exceptionally fine treatment. It will produce a sense of satisfaction inasmuch as it will reinforce the person's decision for choosing to do business with us, versus any number of alternative vendors.

Every contact that occurs between company and customer should be engineered and managed to produce such perceptions consistently and reliably. After implementing a comprehensive quality-service program, one of my clients found that customers started making these kinds of comments when they phoned in:

"You're all so helpful there!"

"Everybody sounds so nice, there. It must be a great place to work."

"I don't think I've ever had a bad phone call with your company!"

In other words, the CSRs had achieved and maintained such a high level of excellence that it became one of the most meaningful satisfactions that customers came to anticipate as they did business with the firm. Great service became part of the product that customers were buying. We welcome this challenging expectation that we'll give—and customers will get—the best possible service, all the time.

Low prices can be offered by nearly everyone, and occasionally technological and performance differences exist between vendors' products. But historically, these kinds of differences among competitors prove to be temporary. A much more enduring source of competitive advantage is created by closely engineering customer service satisfaction.

Because most of our customer-service contacts occur by telephone, I'm going to concentrate our attention on ways that we can use this medium to perform exceptionally well. The next section presents a conversational design that you can carefully manage to assure that your customers not only leave your encounters happy but also "singing" your praises.

THE CUSTOMER SERVICE CALL PATH: A BLUEPRINT FOR PRODUCING PEAK CUSTOMER SATISFACTION BY TELEPHONE

To help improve customer service, I have designed a service routine called the Universal Call Path that can be applied to every telephone conversation. It incorporates many of the elements of great service that we have discussed in this chapter. This process has worked for millions of calls, and it is used by a number of my corporate clients. It guides reps so they can predictably and reliably generate extremely positive reactions from customers. For example, the following results have been reported based on the use of the Universal Call Path.

1. All reps sound consistently nice, helpful, and knowledgeable, call after call.
2. The CSR team sounds uniformly professional.
3. Reps, like musicians in a symphony orchestra, can be easily monitored.
4. Reps are easy to coach, because clear definitions exist of poor, average, good, and excellent work.
5. Calls are shortened, having the effect of reducing costs while increasing customer satisfaction through faster service delivery.
6. Calls consistently conclude on a very positive note.
7. Reps' job satisfaction increases.
8. Training of new reps is faster.

9. Employee compensation is more accurately pegged to performance.
10. "Conflict" calls and other challenging and exceptional conversations are managed in a calm, reliable, and routine manner.

How to Make Beautiful "Music" Together

Before getting into the details of the Universal Call Path, I would like to elaborate on our metaphor of reps as members of a symphony orchestra. When you manage a team of CSRs, think of yourself as a symphony conductor. Each of your representatives has a unique personality, or "instrument," through which he or she expresses him- or herself. So the sounds each rep makes will sound individualized, to some extent. *But your job, as a conductor, is to get all the reps to play the same musical composition at the same time.* They need to be "on the same page"; one person over in the strings section can't be allowed to play a Beethoven piece when everyone is supposed to be focusing on a Mozart composition.

If conductors allowed everyone to play compositions of his or her own choosing, we'd get nothing but noise! The same principle applies to managing customer transactions. Transactions have the potential of becoming deeply satisfying compositions, providing we use some artistry to determine what elements they should contain, so we can appeal to the greatest number of customers. This is what I've tried to achieve with the Universal Call Path. It is a short composition that needs to be played note-for-note. You're the conductor, and your reps are the musicians. Working together, you can accomplish a result that will surprise and delight your customers.

How Can You Be Confident It Will Work?

The Call Path has been tracked carefully over time, to assure that it delivers what it promises. In fact, I do not know of a single company for which the Universal Call Path has failed to improve service outcomes. I'll provide you with thorough operating instructions, so you'll be able to put it to the test.

Why Use a Call Path?

A special mix of events and challenges led to me create the Call Path. For years, I had been in the telephone communications field, as a rep, a manager, and a consultant. In collections and telemarketing work, I had written and used very effective "scripts" for making conversations succinct and persuasive. My Ph.D.

training in communications theory enabled me to conceptualize and design new scripts and conversational strategies, much as an engineer designs machines or an architect designs buildings.

But in customer service, using a telephone script was, and still is, to a large extent a new concept. Customarily, CSRs are left to their own devices to fashion what they consider to be suitable explanations and responses to customers. But by improvising, they frequently fail to meet the challenges they face. On any given call, they could be glib and brilliant, but on the next, they could fall flat on their faces. That's the problem with winging it. It's unreliable.

CSRs usually receive excellent training with respect to their products and company procedures. However, little time is invested in helping them to package what they know into effective communications. When they're under the stress and pressure of incessant calls, the challenge of delivering a lot of content in a smooth, interpersonally satisfying manner can be just too much to handle.

Thus the effectiveness of CSRs becomes unacceptably variable, depending on their moods, their workloads, and the attitudes and challenges that customers present to them. For this reason, they need a communications template that will give them the ability to consistently provide customer satisfaction for each and every caller.

How to Engineer a Service Renaissance

The need for a template was quite apparent to me when a large mutual fund company retained me as a consultant. The "Crash of 1987" had disrupted the securities industry, and many firms had to contend with angry and concerned customers.

In an industry survey of client satisfaction, my client ranked #24 out of a field of 26 participating fund groups. It also was losing employees in droves. I was informed that its employee turnover rate in the CSR group alone was about 100% per year. In customer service, normal turnover is closer to 8–10%.

My mandate was to help produce a service "renaissance." Before I arrived, the CSRs had been put through a good amount of "please-and-thank-you" training, but they weren't saying either—at least very often.

I'm going to outline the specific steps I took to solve my client's problem. Whether you adopt my Call Path or decide to craft your own, replicating my proven protocol may boost your unit's performance.

Step One: Study Customer Transactions

Consultants have an advantage over employees at a given site. We're outsiders, and so we don't take for granted those things that "everybody knows" about "what will or won't work here." If we're good at what we do and we're disciplined, we start our work with what Zen practitioners call "a beginner's mind."

I began at my client's service center simply by observing transactions. I listened to hundreds of conversations, not so much to identify what was wrong with them but to determine what was right.

Step Two: Focus on Success

Then I asked this question:

When are customers happiest with the service they've received?

This was the answer:

Customers are happiest when they think CSRs have gone out of their way for them in getting information, solving a problem, and in making it easier to do business with the company.

My second question:

How do customers express their happiness with CSRs?

Answer:

They express their happiness in three ways: (1) They thank reps in a strong way; (2) they actually "sing" by elevating their voices to new peaks; and (3) they express their intention to do more business with the rep's company.

To my knowledge, no one had ever before identified these three, distinctive signs of customer satisfaction; yet you'll be able to identify them in your best customer conversations.

Step Three: Design a Reliable Method for Increasing Customer Satisfaction

I asked another basic question:

How can we induce customers to feel happy with us all the time?

Here's the answer I came up with:

Always go out of our way for them.

Of course, when I first considered this principle, I believed it was valid but impractical. In most customer service-settings, reps are called on to answer basic questions that don't require Herculean effort.

So, how can we *always* go out of our way for people? In all practicality, it's impossible to do this in every transaction. To illustrate this situation from the point of another business, let's examine how someone might call a brokerage to ask for a quotation on Disney stock. This inquiry can be handled very quickly, and the caller wouldn't want us (the brokerage) to sidetrack into irrelevancies or to complicate the transaction. Yet, at the same time, to instill in a client the highest perception of service, I determined that we should *always seem ready, willing, and able to go out of our way.*

So, we can seem eager to quickly look up the closing quote and then signal to the listener that we're willing to do even more. That way, we'll exceed expectations while sending a positive service message to customers.

But it takes a Call Path protocol to deliberately accomplish this. I'm going to show you how a basic brokerage transaction might go without an effective protocol. Then we'll process the same transaction through the Universal Call Path, which will substantially improve it.

Example: The standard way of handling the price quote would be:
"Hello, Goodman Securities, how may I help you?"
"May I have a quote on Disney, please?"
"Yes, one moment. Disney closed at 45."
"Thank you very much."
"You're welcome. Bye."
"Bye."

This is a plain-vanilla conversation, which happens millions of times every day. It's quick, it isn't offensive, and it gets the job done. *But it doesn't achieve exceptional results with customers. It doesn't surprise and delight them or make them feel special and important.* The same inquiry can *sparkle* if we improve some of its elements. The Universal Call Path will transform this lackluster customer service encounter into a satisfying one.

Example: Here is the Disney inquiry again, handled by the Call Path:

> **"Hello, Goodman Securities, how may I help you?"**
> "May I have a quote on Disney, please?"
> **"Sure, I'll be happy to help you with that. Disney closed at 45, and is there anything else I can help you with?"**
> "No, that's great. Thank you very much."
> **"Well, thank you for doing business with Goodman Securities!"**
> "You bet! Bye."
> "Bye."

At first glance, this conversation doesn't seem to be radically different from the first example, but a close examination will reveal that it is.

What Makes the Call Path Effective?

Let's analyze the preceding Call Path by looking at what's different about it. The greeting is standard. So, the first significant change is ushered in by what I call the Promise of Help. It is the phrase:

> *Sure, I'll be happy to help you with that.*

This phrase is injected into the conversation before the CSR delivers the stock-price information. It is designed to send two crucial messages to customers:

1. *Please be assured that you're going to get what you called for.*
2. *I'm going to take pleasure in helping you.*

Wouldn't it be faster to simply deliver the Disney quote and leave this phrase out? It would seem so, but it doesn't work out that way. Customers are anxious, so they have a tendency to talk too much and to ramble. Specifically, (1) they're concerned that they won't get the information they want, and (2) they're concerned that the CSR will be inept or abrasive. Therefore, anticipating service hassles, customers rehearse their questions while they dial the phone, and then they "spray and pray" all sorts of irrelevant details at the CSR.

By saying, *Sure, I'll be happy to help you with that . . .* we say: (1) You're going to get help; and (2) I'm going to enjoy giving it to you. As a result, clients relax, they let the CSR get down to business, and calls are abbreviated.

But calls are also shorter because the next Call Path segment brings calls to a timely conclusion. I refer to this Call Path element as the *Offer of Additional Help*:

And is there anything else I can help you with?

With the proper timing, this question performs two essential functions.

1. It signals that the business of the call has been completed. Unless a phrase is used to indicate this point, the conversation can ramble and degrade into a sullen sounding conclusion.

2. It volunteers additional help, and, in doing so, it makes a positive impression on the customer. This phrase, when combined with the Promise of Help, conveys the idea that we're willing to go out of our way for the customer.

How Not to Conclude a Call

An inadequate version of the Offer of Additional Help is used in many of today's service conversations. It fails, in part, because it is offered too late. It seems like an insincere afterthought on the part of the rep.

Here's how it usually occurs, in the context of the overall call.

"Hello, Goodman Securities, how may I help you?"

"May I have a quote on Disney, please?"

"Okay, Disney closed at 87."

"That's all I needed."

"Is there anything else I can help you with?"

"No, thanks. Bye."

"Bye."

Calls that conclude like this prevent a number of positive outcomes. They don't induce customers to "sing," and they don't get customers to commit their future business to us.

When we make an Offer of Additional Help with the proper timing, this phrase is woven, seamlessly, into the fabric of the call, like this:

"Sure, I'll be happy to help you with that. Disney closed at 87, and is there anything else I can help you with?"

"No, that's great. Thank you very much."

"Well, thank you for doing business with Goodman Securities!"

"You bet! Bye."

"Bye."

The Volunteering of Help Makes Us Sound Sincere

It is extremely important to seem as if we're volunteering our help. When we do so, we are praiseworthy, because we seem to be going beyond the call of duty. When we hesitate, we seem reluctant and less than wholehearted in our desire to achieve more.

So, when we're late in introducing our Offer of Additional Help, our *words* seem to be asking if there's something else we can do, but our *timing* belies our words and implies "I don't really mean what I'm saying. Let's end this call, right now!" Consequently, customers won't feel they've been mishandled, but they won't feel they've been treated exceptionally well, either, which won't induce them to commit to us for the long term. If one of our competitors comes along and uses the equivalent of the Call Path, clients defect to them, opting to go where the communication rewards are.

Done well, the Offer of Additional Help saves phone time. It signals, in a very pleasant manner, that the call is coming to an end, thus reducing the temptation of reps and customers to ramble. At the same time, it promises the customer, "I won't hang up until you have been completely satisfied." So, there is no downside to using this phrase as instructed. It says, "If there isn't anything else to be transacted, we're out of here! But if there is, then please, take your time." This is a win/win message strategy. It enables reps to invest additional time only with those who really need it. Otherwise, it frees the line for the next customer call.

As mentioned, the Offer of Additional Help sets up what we call "singing" and customer commitment dynamics as the call comes to a close. To appreciate how this works, we need to focus on another variable that we strategically employ: the rep's *pitch*, or *voice tone.*

A Recipe for Using the Best Tones of Voice

I'm going to provide you with some critical instructions for how a rep's voice should sound as she is using the Call Path. As a general rule, her pitch, or the highs and lows of her voice, will be calibrated closely to her text.

Here's how it works. As she proceeds through the Call Path, she first does the Greeting; that is, she says hello, announces her company or department's name and her name, and she asks how can she be of help.

Hello, Xerox Customer Service, this is Shirley— How may I help you?

As I noted, there is nothing remarkable about the text of the greeting. But a new tonal instruction that I'll share with you makes the greeting sound especially sincere. Before I do, let me point out an important fact that we know about how customers interpret tones. *If our tones are not synchronized with our words, we'll seem phony, or even sarcastic. This can turn clients off, or make them laugh at the incongruity.* It's worth the effort to match our tones to our words.

The Proper Tone for the Greeting

Here's how we should accomplish this task in our Greeting. When the rep asks, "How may I help you?" the word "you" should be elevated in pitch, above the words, "How may I help . . ." This change in pitch sends a signal to the listener that says, "I really want to help—I'm looking forward to it."

Let me emphasize that this is not the way 99.9% of reps spontaneously deliver this line. What they do is put their tones on a *default setting*. Instead of really thinking about the best way to tonally express a phrase, they adopt an arbitrary, sing-song melody that can make them sound listless or bored.

In most Greetings, reps will emphasize the word "Help." So, with respect to pitch, the phrase looks like this:

> *help*
>
> *How*
>
> *may I*   *you?*

Note how the tone dips at the end of the phrase. This is unfortunate, because it makes reps seem less than truly sincere about helping.

Here's how the phrase should sound:

> *you?*
>
> *How may I*
>
>   *help*

This tonal technique won't completely make sense to you until you prove the difference to yourself.

Exercise: Using a tape recorder, perform the Greeting. Don't bother recording an actual call at this point.

First, record yourself saying, "How may I help you?" as you normally say it. Then, repeat the line as I've indicated most folks do it, with the pitch of the word "help" elevated. Without stopping the recorder, then practice saying the line as I've instructed you to do it. You may find that you experience a little difficulty in breaking out of your accustomed patterns. That's to be expected. It takes many rehearsals of the correct tonal progression, before you, or your reps, can change vocal habits. Next, play back the tape, imagining the different effects the various greetings would have on you, if you were the customer. I'm sure you'll hear some significant differences.

Later, I'll ask you to record actual conversations, and you'll hear how real customers react to the various pitch patterns they hear from reps. At that point, when you have concrete proof of the validity of what I'm saying, you'll probably become a believer in the power of tone of voice to change the outcomes of conversations!

The Proper Tone for the Promise of Help

To bring the Call Path to life, you'll need to manage all three crucial, script-related variables: *text, tone, and timing.* Let's look at how the Promise of Help needs to be performed, tonally, for it to "ring true" to clients. Basically, we're going to do exactly the same thing we did in the Greeting. The pitch of the last word of the Promise of Help needs to soar above the rest:

                                                                        that.

                                                you with

Sure, I'll be happy

                            to help

The usual pattern, which I urge you to avoid, looks like this:

                        happy

Sure, I'll be   *to help*

                                                        you with

                                                                that.

When performed properly, this phrase communicates the idea that we really do want to be of help. It says, "I'm looking forward to assisting you!" and it makes the customer feel that her call isn't an imposition or an interruption.

After hearing the Promise of Help, it's common for customers to respond: "Oh, great!" which signals that we've aroused a degree of satisfaction and relief before we have even answered the person's question or responded to her concern.

The Proper Tone for the Offer of Additional Help

Similar to the Greeting and the Promise of Help, the Offer of Additional Help ends on a high pitch. But we're going to reach that pitch by doing something that I refer to as vocal stair-stepping. The tonal pattern of the Offer of Additional Help looks like this:

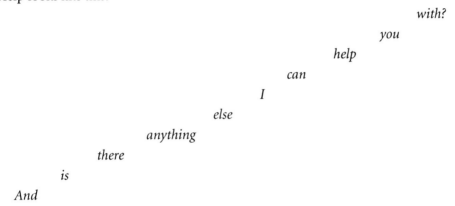

Using this pattern is essential if you want your customers to "sing," because it gets the rep to sing first. Then, the customer imitates the rep. But "singing" will be much less frequent if we say the Offer of Additional Help the wrong way, like this:

```
                        else
          anything              I
      there                  can
    is                        help
And                               you
                                     with?
```

Can you see how anticlimactic this version is? It makes the rep seem less genuine. Moreover, when the rep sounds "down in the dumps," the customer will likely adopt this mood and go away with an uneasy and unfulfilled feeling about the transaction.

The True Value of Keeping Clients Aboard: The Call Path's Recommitment Line

So far we have examined three of the four components of the Universal Call Path: the Greeting, the Promise of Help, and the Offer of Additional Help. Now we turn to the fourth component, the Recommitment Line. Reflect for a moment on the significance of inducing customers to pledge their loyalty to us. Can you imagine how much more solid and secure our customer bases would be if they consisted of strong supporters instead of potentially fickle friends?

You've probably heard the statistic that it costs four times as much to earn a new client than to keep an existing customer on the books. If we can retain just a small proportion of customers who would otherwise leave the fold, efforts to implement the Call Path will be handsomely rewarded. *Keeping customers happy and loyal is a power that we can exercise in each and every customer service encounter.*

Customer commitment can be viewed as an anchor. With each "wave," or conversation, the anchor of commitment can dig more deeply into the sand, or it can become progressively dislodged. If we swamp our clients with too many negative waves, we'll cast them adrift, and they'll eventually reach our rivals. To avoid this, I've fashioned a Recommitment Line and inserted it into the Call Path. It tells customers how much we appreciate them, and it gives them a chance to tell us how much they appreciate us. In the example I provided earlier, I said:

Well, thank you for doing business with Goodman Securities!

This line is designed to get the customer to reply with a phrase such as, "You bet!" or "Sure thing!" or "Anytime!" In other words, we want them to say the equivalent of this:

I will definitely buy from you again.

We should praise the customer for doing what we want them to do—that is, reward us with their business. We want their phone calls only as a means to accomplishing this end. Therefore, we avoid repeating the cliché "Well, thank you for calling." We don't want them to think "Okay, I'll call again." We want them to say "Okay, I'll give you more business!" This is a much stronger response, don't you agree? *Our Recommitment Line gives them something significant to recommit to.*

Recommitment and the Big Picture

Fundamentally, the task of sales and marketing people is to get customers to commit to doing business with them, and the task of customer service personnel is to get those customers to recommit. The first function gets them, and the second one keeps them coming back, again and again.

If a CSR doesn't try to recommit a client, it is as foolish and wasteful as a salesperson failing to "close," failing to ask a customer for his business. Asking for recommitment shouldn't be optional, because it is essential to the proper maintenance and growth of the organization.

The Proper Tone for the Recommitment Line

The tonal structure of the Recommitment Line is exactly the same as for the Offer of Additional Help. It stair-steps upward to a crescendo:

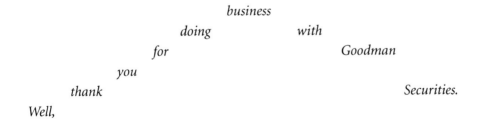

Reps will be tempted to utter this line with the same default settings I mentioned when I discussed the Offer of Additional Help. They'll want to peak on the word "business." This would be anticlimactic and would not encourage customer recommitment. Here's an example of a wrong tonal pattern:

Troubleshooting Your Call Path Questions

Correctly used, the Call Path can become an awesome piece of communication machinery. Reps glide through conversations. They consistently sound upbeat and positive, and customers feel they're getting special treatment.

Thousands of CSRs have used the Call Path, in millions of customer contacts, with great success. But you probably have some questions and concerns about it. I'll try to address the major ones.

"What happens in long calls? Does the Call Path still work?"

Absolutely. In almost all calls, you'll want to include its four main components. The Greeting comes first, which gets the customer to reveal why she called. You'll introduce the Promise of Help immediately after the customer states her business or asks a question. You'll then handle the customer's issues and wrap up the conversation with the Offer of Additional Help and your Recommitment Line.

"What if clients have complex questions or concerns?"

The caller might say: "My computer just crashed, and I don't know what to do." Will the Promise of Help work in this case?

Absolutely. In fact, when you're facing a big challenge or an angry customer, the Promise of Help should ease tensions right away. In the case of a crashed computer, the rep should simply follow the Promise of Help with a number of questions to diagnose the computer's problem. This could take quite a bit of time. In fact, the CSR or Technical Support Rep may have to go back and forth with the customer, trying various "fixes," until the machine is up and running again. At this point, the rep should return to the Call Path, and say:

"And is there anything else I can help you with?"

Assuming there aren't additional issues, the customer will "sing," aware of all of the help she has received. And then, just as the Call Path provides, the rep will finish with:

"Well, thank you for doing business with Acme Computers!"

"When can reps choose their own words?"

Complex calls usually include a large, unscripted portion that I refer to as "The Great Middle." This is the time that reps deliver the "content" of their help. They provide company or product information or probe to determine what the client's problems are all about.

Reps and managers have discretion regarding the length of the Great Middle. In Technical Support departments, reps will often have written guides that they'll be able to follow to efficiently troubleshoot and resolve product breakdowns. Reps can then bridge-back to the Call Path and conclude the conversation on a high note.

"Are there times when you don't want to stick to the Call Path?"

Having worked with numerous companies, I can honestly say that there are very few circumstances for which I would counsel against using the Call Path. But exceptions do occur. Usually, they'll leap out at you.

Recently, a rep at a manufacturing company received a call from an admitted competitor who was trying to do a little industrial espionage to learn some of the manufacturer's secrets. The rep told me, "Gary, I didn't use the Promise of Help, because I felt it wouldn't be appropriate to say, 'Sure, I'll be happy to help you to rip us-off!'"

She used good judgment, and I thanked her for sharing the experience, because I have so few examples of when the Call Path should be avoided.

"Should the Call Path be used in super-brief, 'transfer calls?'"

When the customer reaches Mary but really needs to be transferred to Bill, should Mary say, "Sure, I'll be happy to transfer you to Bill, who is at extension 22?"

Why not? It certainly makes an otherwise bland encounter more pleasant, doesn't it?

Case in Point—Le Hermitage Hotel in Beverly Hills: Incoming calls are handled in a very charming way at Le Hermitage Hotel, Beverly Hills. When I was arranging to do seminars at that site, I called the hotel and asked for the Catering Manager. Without missing a beat, the operator responded with a very pleasant, "My pleasure!" Then she promptly connected my call. This is a friendly, yet elegant method for being connected to another extension, don't you think? When I first heard it, I was very pleased!

This is an example of how a simple phrase can surprise and delight customers. Le Hermitage demonstrates that it really doesn't take too much to make the simplest of transactions more pleasant.

"Does the Call Path lose its effectiveness if the same customer hears it again and again?"

My experience indicates that the effectiveness of the Call Path is cumulative. Through repeated exposure to it, clients increasingly perceive reps as being helpful and caring. This impression is reinforced, by design. We use the word "help" at least three times in each Call Path:

- How may I **help** you?
- Sure, I'll be happy to **help** you with that.
- And is there anything else I can **help** you with?

So it's not a surprise that, in the many letters of praise that my clients receive, most of the writers mention how helpful the CSRs are.

But there is another, significant reason the Call Path gains in power with repeated use. It injects a great amount of courtesy into every conversation, and I'm confident your customers will never tire of being treated so well!

This chapter has defined the basic elements of great customer service, both conceptually and operationally. It also provided the example of the Universal Call Path for establishing excellent telephone relations with customers and described its four components: Greeting, Promise of Help, Offer of Additional Help, and Recommitment Line. In the next chapter, we'll discuss the best methods for monitoring the performance of your representatives and associates to assure that (1) they're doing the right things, (2) they're doing things right, and (3) they're being justly judged and rewarded for their fine work.

The Anatomy of Service Success: Identifying the Eighteen Communication Factors That Promote Top Customer Service

In Chapter 1 you saw how four communication components can be woven into a powerful customer service support template called the Universal Call Path, which can make customer telephone calls achieve excellent results. You may now be asking about what other factors contribute to great customer service. There are eighteen additional factors that affect customer-service quality. These factors, together with the four Call Path elements, will provide the backbone of the call measurement system, which I'll introduce later in this book.

For now, we're going to more precisely define how successful customer service reps communicate. If someone from your Human Resources department asked you to describe an ideal CSR, I hope you'd refer them to this chapter.

Here is a preview of the eighteen key communication characteristics that we're going to examine:

1. General Demeanor/Cheerfulness

2. Courtesy

3. Articulation

4. Speed

5. Pitch

6. Volume

7. Calibration

8. Vocabulary

9. Grammar

10. Energy

11. Quickness

12. Accuracy

13. Appropriateness/Relevance

14. Organization

15. Transitions

16. Empathy/Supportiveness

17. Listening/Active Listening

18. Evoking the Right Responses

1. EXCELLENT CSRs: THEY'RE POSITIVE AND CHEERFUL

I manage my daughter's Little League Softball team, the Wildcats. Fourteen 9–12 year olds are quite a lot to handle, I can tell you! But there are certain individuals who are an utter delight to behold. One of them is another manager's daughter. Whenever she does anything related to baseball, she just beams with a positive attitude.

How can I tell she's so positive? It's easy. It's written all over her face. If she's playing the infield, she'll smile. If she's in the batter's box, she'll smile. If she's on base or in the dugout, she's still smiling! I can't help smiling whenever I see her. Positive attitudes work like that. Emanate positivity, and it will reflect right back to you.

CSRs can smile as well—even if they're speaking on the phone. Generally, their smiles and their enthusiasm for their work will be communicated through their voices. It's fairly straightforward to define how positive people sound during calls:

They sound upbeat.

This means that the ends of their sentences and phrases move up in tone, at least a little. As you know, we've already emphasized this rising tonal pattern in the four Call Path elements, by saying that the following words should sound especially upbeat:

*How may I help **you**?*

*Sure, I'll be happy to help you with **that**.*

*And is there anything else I can help you **with**?*

*Well, thank you for doing business with **us**!*

The principle of General Demeanor/Cheerfulness provides a guideline for reps to sound upbeat when they're on their own, during the Great Middle of calls. The principle states: Make your voice tones *crest* instead of decline.

If a rep's voice hasn't crested in a considerable amount of time, she's probably coming across as dull and disinterested in her work. Or worse, if her tones decline, she's going to sound as though she's down in the dumps.

In the previous chapter I mentioned that we can't always hire the most spectacular people—and this includes naturally cheerful people. But all reps have it in their power to act cheerfully by modulating their voices in an upbeat way. Positive- and optimistic-sounding people make customers want to transact more and more business, so it pays off to make sure we sound upbeat.

2. GREAT REPS ARE CONSISTENTLY COURTEOUS

You might think that, if you hire the right people, they'll automatically and consistently be courteous to customers. But even the most considerate folks need to be reminded occasionally to say "please" and "thank you."

As a general rule, we don't thank our customers enough for giving us the privilege of doing business with them. As we do our loved ones, we take customers for granted. When we do that, another vendor comes along and through a showing of politeness and gracious communications steals the "affections" of our customers.

The best defense against a competitor's siren song is to continuously "court" our own clients. This means making great efforts to show them all the attention that we would pay to a new source of business, and it means we should thank customers many times in the same transaction, if at all possible. For example, imagine we're on the phone and we need to leave the line for a second. We wouldn't want to just say, "One moment, please" and park the customer on hold. It would be much better to say:

"I need to retrieve some information for you, and it'll take about sixty seconds. May I ask you to hold?"

("Sure.")

"Thank you, I'll be right back."

Asking permission before leaving the line shows courtesy, and one should thank the customer for giving permission. These verbal gestures demonstrate that we're sensitive to the feelings of customers and that we regard them with great respect.

As you'll see later on, we'll measure courtesy by determining whether an appropriate "please" or "thank you" has been used. Usually, their absence is conspicuous and can be easily measured.

3. ARTICULATION IS ESSENTIAL TO PROVIDING A GOOD SERVICE EXPERIENCE

Articulation is a frequently misunderstood term because it is used in so many contexts. When Bill says, "Mary sounded so articulate!" what is he saying? Usually, this statement means that the articulate individual uses appropriate words in a smooth and impressive way. Important as this skill may be, it isn't what we mean when we speak about articulation. For us, *articulation is the full formation of words so they are completely understandable to a listener of reasonable sensibilities.*

An articulate person uses his or her articulators—the lips, teeth, and tongue—to utter clear and comprehensible words. Good articulators don't slur their words. Instead of being lazy speakers, they take pains to make sure their pronunciation is clear.

So, if they are saying the word "articulation," each syllable comes through:

ar-ti-cu-la-tion

They don't merge syllables:

ar-ti-cla-tion

Note the difference. It's significant, I'm sure you'll agree, and we're discussing only a single word. Imagine what can happen if a speaker slurs a slew of words, sentence after sentence. It becomes a lot of work to simply decode what is being said!

There is another important reason to fully form our words. When we do, we sound much more intelligent. Having said this, I should caution you about overdoing it. We don't want to laboriously overarticulate by slowly punching out every syllable, as if it were a separate word. This would make us sound stilted or effete, and customers could take offense.

How can you tell if you or your reps are articulating properly? For now, let me say that using a tape recorder will help you to detect good as well as poor articulation. Moreover, you'll also know that customers are having difficulty comprehending reps when they constantly say, "What?" and "Can you repeat that please?"

4. WATCH OUT FOR SPEED BUMPS!

Two types of speakers can be especially frustrating: slow talkers and fast talkers. But what constitutes slow or fast is a subjective issue about which reasonable people can disagree.

Let me give you an example, which I call the "Gary, Larry, and Harry Story." One day, I called a friend of mine in Kentucky. We had a nice chat, but I was a little frustrated because Larry seemed to prefer speaking at a rate that was a lot slower than my own. Being a communications person, I got in touch with my desire to speed him up, and I harnessed this impulse. By the time our call ended, we were both blissfully taking our good, old time, and we said a friendly goodbye.

My next call was to Harry, a friend in New York City. I opened the conversation with an expansive, "How're you doing, Harry?" and without hesitating, he barked back, "Get to the point!" Quickly, I discarded my mellowness and got down to business.

The moral to the story is that "speed" is relative and that there are regional differences in acceptable rates of speech. But now that I've said this, I should also say that there is a happy middle ground that appeals to most Americans: *It is the range of 100–150 words per minute.*

If you and your reps communicate with customers within this standard, you'll probably find that you're safely in the comfort zone of most listeners. Occasionally, you'll encounter the Larrys and Harrys, who are at bipolar extremes, but they'll be exceptions to the rule.

Measuring vocal rates is an objective and relatively easy process, which you'll learn about in a later chapter.

5. HOW TO HAVE PERFECT PITCH

How do radio announcers capture and keep our attention? Yes, some are gifted with especially resonant voices, but that is mainly a happy genetic accident. Either we have marvelous "pipes," as they say, or we don't.

Many radio pros with average voices make them sound exceptional by working on various tonal patterns. One kind of pattern involves what we call *pitch*. As we mentioned in Chapter 1, pitch consists of the highs and lows in one's vocal range. Unless we have received excellent voice or speech coaching, we normally wouldn't give much thought to the pitch-patterns we repeatedly use. But to realize one's full potential as a CSR, we should pay at least some attention to this factor.

As a general rule, we use only a very narrow part of our vocal bandwidth. We don't reach many highs or lows, and so one might say that we usually speak in a monotone. *Monotone* means "one tone." The problem with a monotonic voice is that it is boring. This is occasionally good—say, if you're an air traffic controller. If a flight is coming in for a precarious landing, you don't want to sound overly excited. Instead, you want to sound super steady and rock solid.

However, when we're conducting everyday business, we want to impress customers as being warm and fully dimensioned human beings. Therefore, we should use a broad range of expressiveness to give the impression that we're real, genuine, complete people.

A "perfect" pitch pattern is one that introduces *variety* into one's speech. By introducing more highs and lows, as if your voice were a musical instrument, you'll accomplish this end, and people will enjoy their conversations with you. They'll feel they know you, and this is a comfort to them.

6. IF YOU WANT TO GET SOMEONE'S ATTENTION, JUST . . .

Varying the volume with which we speak—the softness and the loudness—will also make our conversations more meaningful and enjoyable to customers. As you may suspect, we also tend to use a monotonic style when it comes to the vocal intensity with which we speak.

There is an easy fix for this tendency. Deliberately belt out a given word or phrase, especially if you want the listener to perk up and get the point you're trying to make. Or, when you want to gain or regain someone's attention, as the perfume commercial says, "just whisper."

In fact, nearly any departure from the monotonic norm will make your delivery distinctive, and this will capture the customer's attention. This is just the right prescription to make you more compelling, and therefore, more influential.

Again, the principle that we're emphasizing here is vocal variety. This doesn't mean that everything needs to stand out in our speech. On the contrary, I'm suggesting that we make enough of our comments sound different so that we avoid the flat voice that implies "Gee, I'm so bored with this."

7. CALIBRATE YOUR CONVERSATIONS

There is a subtle give-and-take sequence to effective conversations. In social encounters, you might say that a good chat is one in which both persons share the communications channel on a 50/50 basis. In other words, each individual will strive to talk 50% of the time and listen during the remaining 50%. Neither person dominates the channel—at least in mutually enjoyable social situations. In business, we might find that other ratios apply. For instance, an angry or upset customer might need ample time to "cathart," or let off steam. Obviously, when this happens, CSRs are not going to try to insist on their 50% of talking time.

In contrast, if a customer is asking for technical support in using a software program, the rep may have to hold forth for a considerable time to explain how to use the program. This is normal. So, we can't say that a fixed ratio of talking time is appropriate to business conversations.

But we are still vitally interested in permitting both parties the chance to comment freely, without feeling that they're being overwhelmed by the other. This is where "calibration" comes in as a communications standard. A well-calibrated conversation is one that flows freely. Neither party talks when the other is talking or is silent while the other is silent. Therefore, there aren't any annoying pauses or overlaps in the discussion. Participants aren't fighting with each other to get a word in edgewise.

It is up to the CSR to calibrate the call, so that it is a comfortable, give-and-take encounter. No one likes to be cut off in mid-sentence or feel that he is speaking into a void, from which no feedback is forthcoming. Both of these events would be considered calibration problems that should be avoided.

8. VOCABULARY: THE ART OF USING THE RIGHT WORDS

When most of us were in school, we had lists of vocabulary words that we were required to learn. Presumably, by having more terms at our disposal, we could understand and express ideas with greater capability.

You may be pleased to hear that we're concerned about a rep's vocabulary as well, but not with respect to the quantity of terms she knows. We're more interested in whether a rep uses the right word for the situation. For example, a mutual fund representative told a customer that he would be receiving a statement of his account once, annually, instead of twice yearly, as had been the custom. The rep said, "They'll be sending you a statement once, annually, in December."

The word "They'll" was inappropriate. He should have used "We'll," as in "We'll be sending you a statement once, annually, in December." Because the rep was new on the job, he still thought of the company as a "they," as some outside entity. For him, the company had not yet become a "we," as it would if he had felt more highly identified with it.

9. GRAMMAR COUNTS!

A few decades ago, elementary schools were also known as "grammar schools," because there was tremendous emphasis placed on teaching this topic. Grammar consists of the rules and conventions that should be followed when we speak a particular language. For example, one such rule is that subjects and verbs in sentences should agree:

He doesn't like spinach is grammatical.

He don't like spinach isn't grammatical.

Millions of Americans do not use appropriate grammar. These include college graduates, who should know better. Some of their transgressions are relatively minor. For example, it is idiomatically common to use adjectives instead of adverbs:

She didn't play fairly is grammatical.

She didn't play fair isn't grammatical.

We're concerned about using correct grammar because it reflects on our own credibility as well as on that of our companies. In an era of heightened sophistication, customers are becoming more educated and more demanding. They don't want to feel that they're entrusting their accounts to bozos, yet we could inadvertently convey that impression if we speak poorly.

So, when we measure the effectiveness of reps, grammar will count.

10. ELECTRIFY CUSTOMERS WITH YOUR ENERGY

How do you feel when you have phoned into a customer service and the rep you have reached sounds lethargic or listless? Does that make you feel that you made a wise choice in choosing to do business with that firm?

Reps who radiate a lot of energy make you believe your call is welcome. For example, the receptionist at the Orlando Marriott hotel bellows out this greeting:

It's a great day at the Orlando Marriott!

I, for one, believe her. Her sunny mood makes me imagine that there is nothing less than a dazzling blue sky in that resort venue. If I'm booking a seminar there, I feel that I'm already basking in the glow of their hospitality. In short, through her energy, the receptionist conveys the impression that the Orlando Marriott is nothing less than the very best place on earth, for anything and everything.

Now, if she were answering the phone for the Eternity Funeral Parlor, she'd be in big trouble with her dazzling, million-watt greeting. But, I'm sure you'd agree, there are strikingly few organizations where showing a low level of energy is better than exhibiting a high one.

11. JACK BE NIMBLE, JACK BE QUICK!

Quickness is the ability of a rep to answer a question or supply information in a timely way. It is a reflection of her knowledge of products and procedures that comes through, contact after contact. A rep who isn't quick enough is one who seems to take an inordinate amount of time to deliver the information or the response that a customer requires. We don't penalize reps for slowness if it is caused by problems that are beyond their control. For example, if their computer systems aren't responding, they can't be justly criticized for that.

12. LET'S DELIVER ACCURATE INFORMATION

When I first designed my measurement system for customer service, managers and reps were both relieved to discover that I had included a provision for evaluating the quality of information being dispensed. It is the factor we call accuracy.

Accuracy concerns the truthfulness, completeness, and validity of the information that the rep delivers to customers. For instance, if a customer calls in and asks about the hours that a store is open on a weekend, it can be a critical gaffe if the rep declares "We're open until 8" if the establishment really closes at 6 or at 7. Imagine how inconvenient it would be for a customer to drive a great distance only to discover that the rep had misinformed her. If you think this is a remote possibility, let me share the following story with you.

The laptop that I'm using to write this book had a problem with the floppy drive. So, I took it into the authorized repair shop around 10 a.m., and it was promised to me at 3. Now, this establishment is about 10 miles from my office. I arrived at 3, and I was told to return at 5, which I did. At 5, I was told it would *definitely* be ready at 7 p.m.—closing time. Finally, it was ready as promised.

But I had to return no fewer than three times to retrieve my machine! The technician's inaccurate predictions made me drive 60 miles and waste about an hour and a half on the freeway. Would you say she should be admonished about the importance of delivering accurate information to clients?

Accuracy—and the lack of it—reflects on the quality of a company's training and learning processes. If numerous reps are discovered to be misstating facts to the detriment of clients, then steps can be taken to supplement their knowledge. Even the slightest inaccuracy can impeach the credibility of a company. For instance, when I was taking lunch at the local mall, I stopped at a well-known department store. I browsed through the men's shirts and found an attractive style, but I couldn't find a 36–37-inch sleeve length. I asked the sales rep if she could locate one for me at a sister store, and she nodded. Then I asked, "And if you do, they'll send it over here, right?"

"Oh, no!" she exclaimed. "You'll need to go to that store to pick it up."

This sounded preposterous. Nordstrom, which I mentioned in the first chapter, will go to the ends of the earth to find what I want, and once they have it in hand, they'll even deliver it to my door. This other store was telling me that I'd have to personally waste my time tracking down a single shirt.

I was blown away by the difference. And then it hit me: The sales clerk was probably supplying me with inaccurate information. Later I spoke to another clerk who assured me that it was normal procedure to find an item and then to have it delivered to the store that had requested it.

But a lot of credibility had been lost. This gaffe led me to infer that I was better served by giving my business to stores that trained their people better.

13. APPROPRIATENESS: RAMBLIN' REPS SHOULD BE ROPED IN

If there is one occupational hazard that seems to befall experienced CSRs it is this: They learn so many details about their products, services, and companies that they feel compelled to bring as many of them as possible into each and every conversation.

At the same time, the newest reps tend to leave out critical details because they're nervous, in a hurry, or ill informed. So, we developed a measure that would address this issue. The measure is Appropriateness/Relevance. If reps over-talk or overexplain, they are said to be irrelevant. If they under-talk, or under-explain, they are said to be communicating inappropriately. This is an extremely handy measure.

Many companies—and possibly yours—assess reps based on the length of their calls. There is nothing wrong with this, *if*, and this is a big if, reps are instructed in methods for controlling call length. One method is the Appropriateness/Relevance measure. It helps the manager to point out exactly when the rep is overexplaining and therefore when he is wasting valuable phone time.

Of course, it stands to reason that some reps, especially in large service centers, will be too brief, and even curt, as they handle their calls. Managers can quite easily use the Appropriateness/Relevance measure to point out when and where they are undercommunicating.

In a phone call that I taped for training purposes, a mutual fund rep, who was new on the job, fell into the trap of underexplaining a crucial point to a client. When he asked when he would see his next dividend, she merely replied:

"On the fifteenth."

He chimed in to clarify her statement: "Of December?" The rep replied, "Yes, the 15th of December." Customers are picky about hearing complete answers, especially when the answers pertain to matters of money!

14. BE ORGANIZED: STATE YOUR POINT, GIVE THE EVIDENCE, STATE YOUR POINT AGAIN (P.E.P.)

The Call Path offers a central advantage to reps: It makes them sound very organized. This is a huge plus, because research tells us that organized people seem more credible, and credible people are more persuasive. So, it pays to sound as organized as possible. Many reps get into trouble because they don't know how to structure improvised conversation.

I'm going to share with you a speech format that enables reps to come across as being super-logical and to-the-point in almost all circumstances. It can even help them to think on their feet when they're being attacked by rude customers. It is called the *P.E.P.* (*Point Evidence Point*) Formula. It's easy to learn and to use for these reasons:

1. It has only three parts.

2. It is immediately applicable to most conversations.

3. It can be written down or be improvised, completely from scratch.

So, once more, it's really easy to learn and to use!

In fact, I just delivered a P.E.P. talk to you! Here's what I did. I started by making a **point**. I said:

The P.E.P. formula is really easy to learn and to use.

Next, I supported that **point** with three pieces of **evidence**. I said:

1. *It has only three parts.*

2. *It is immediately applicable to most conversations.*

3. *It can be written down or be improvised, completely from scratch.*

Then, I concluded my talk with roughly the same point with which I started. I said:

So, once more, it's really easy to learn and to use.

Let's put it all together, so you can read it as a coherent whole.

Point:	*The P.E.P. formula is really easy to learn and to use.*
Evidence:	*1. It has only three parts.*
	2. It is immediately applicable to most conversations.
	3. It can be written down or be improvised, completely from scratch.
Point:	*So, once more, it's really easy to learn and to use.*

Now, let's put the P.E.P formula to use in an actual customer service situation. Let's say you charge a restocking fee to accept returned merchandise. Customers may balk when they hear that they'll have to pay it, so reps need to explain its purpose in a manner that will be agreeable to clients.

Without a device such as P.E.P., it is likely that reps may handle one call well but mishandle the next one. To prevent this problem, you can prepare a P.E.P. response to the customer's challenge: "Why do I have to pay a restocking fee?"

Point:	*We have a modest restocking fee because:*
Evidence:	*1. It enables us to recapture some, but not all, of the costs that we incur by handling the same items twice.*
	2. It encourages our customers to plan their purchases so they don't end up overstocked or understocked.
	3. We believe it's more helpful and flexible than promoting a rule that all sales "are final."
Point:	*So, that's why we have a modest restocking fee, and is there anything else I can help you with?*

P.E.P. formulas can also help a rep to seem organized. That's why I recommend that managers use some time in their meetings with reps to brainstorm P.E.P. "capsules." These are quick informational talks on various aspects of products and services. They can also be used to explain policies, as in the restocking fee example.

For example, they can be used to justify price increases, to explain that there will be continuity after a merger or an acquisition, or to handle nearly any informational or persuasive challenge that reps may face. Armed with the belief that they can remain organized in nearly any situation, reps will be able to project confidence and a professional demeanor.

15. EFFECTIVE TRANSITIONS ARE A CHARACTERISTIC OF THE BEST COMMUNICATORS

Have you ever noticed that people who seem at ease in social situations are often those who are able to carry on conversations on a wide range of topics without using long pauses or hesitations? What they have done, consciously or unconsciously, is master the art of using effective *transitions* to bridge from one idea or topic to the next.

As is the case so often in service encounters, we need to reassert our agenda for the call after a customer has wrested it away from us. How can we interrupt her and get back on track without seeming to be abrupt or impolite? This is where transition phrases come in handy. Most of them follow a similar format. They start with the word, "Well" and end with the word "but." Here are some examples:

Well, I appreciate that, but . . .

Well, I understand that, but . . .

Well, I know what you mean, but . . .

Well, I respect that, but . . .

Well, I'd be surprised if you were at this point, but . . .

So, let's say someone has hijacked your conversation. He is telling you all about his vacation in the mountains, and your life is slowly passing before you. You can makeup your own transition to regain control:

Gee, that sounds like a great trip, but I wanted to mention something before I forget . . .

(By the way, I'd raise my tone on the word "trip" to make the phrase sound positive.)

Transition phrases will help you to move conversations along, save time, and stay on track. So, give them a try!

16. CUSTOMERS WANT MORE THAN INFORMATION—THEY ALSO WANT OUR EMPATHY AND SUPPORTIVENESS

As you know, customer service involves much more than the simple conveyance of information or the routine handling of transactions. If it were only about these mundane tasks, CSRs could be replaced by the Internet or by Interactive Voice Response phone capabilities.

When customers communicate with us, they also want human satisfaction. They want to perceive empathy for their circumstances and supportiveness for their goals. How can we come across as empathic and supportive? I think the following examples and discussion should illustrate the point.

Example: Starbucks Order. When I was having a Starbucks coffee the other morning, an interesting thing happened. A gentleman ordered a few pounds of beans for gifts. In a loud voice, he issued exacting interactions for packaging his purchase, so it would remain fresh. He wanted double bags, and he wouldn't settle for the ordinary, paper ones. He insisted on receiving plastic coffee bags. Every eye in the place was focused on him and on the three or four helpers who were transfixed by this transaction.

The manager was obviously peeved that this fellow had so many unusual requirements. I could sense that she was just waiting for him to cross the line and become abusive, so she could have the pleasure of straightening him out.

But Dawn, the person who waited on him, was very patient. When she didn't understand his requests, she asked for clarification, and then she calmly told him what his options were for obtaining certain styles of bags. He got what he wanted, and a crisis was averted. Dawn applied lots of communication "lubricating oil" to this fellow's gnashing gears. She listened, gave feedback, and she didn't "awfulize" about the man's demanding specifications.

I got the feeling that Dawn believed that this gentleman's exceptional requests weren't abnormal at all. She embodied an attitude that said: "Of course you want special treatment. Our customers are special, and you're going to receive it. So what if it takes three times as long to get your order right!"

Example: The Franklin Mint Strikes Service "Gold." I'd like to share another story that illustrates how a potentially unpleasant event was transformed by a smart representative into a positive outcome. As I was walking through the Glendale Galleria shopping mall, I stopped at the Franklin Mint store. It has a beautiful front window, all decked out with limited edition ceramic plates. A big fellow was looking at one of them, when his hand unexpectedly slipped. The plate wobbled out of his hand and crashed into the Plexiglas display panels, sending shock waves into the air.

Suddenly, all eyes turned to this fellow. Everyone expected a nasty confrontation between the clerks and this poor chap. But what's remarkable is the fact that this didn't happen at all. Swiftly, the store's Assistant Manager came forward and said to the profusely apologetic fellow, "Don't worry. These things happen, and it's not your fault."

I breathed a sigh of relief that he wasn't going to be embarrassed any further by the staff. Right after hearing these soothing words, he offered to pay for the broken plate, but the manager said, "You don't have to do that, but I'll be happy to help you to find something you like!"

A very positive outcome was forged from a crisis. Do you think that fellow will ever forget the Assistant Manager's generosity and gracious attitude? My guess is that she earned a customer for life!

Some Do's and Don'ts for Preventing and Reducing Conflict

The Franklin Mint and Starbucks associates did an admirable job of defusing conflict before it could ignite. They concentrated on *fixing problems* instead of *fixing the blame.*

The coffee customer was asking for a lot, and compared to other customers, he was loud and somewhat brusque. The rep could have focused on his brusque personality and communication style instead of focusing on how to fulfill his requests. She could have reacted defensively to him, thinking: "You can't treat me this way!" Instead, she responded in a task-oriented, supportive way. The customer was made to feel that he is a valued customer whose requests are just as reasonable as anyone else's. In other words, the Starbucks person didn't perceive this gentleman's behavior as a personal threat.

Similarly, the person at the Franklin Mint store didn't send a signal that said, "You broke my plates!" or "Look at the mess you made in my store!" She eased his embarrassment and allowed him to save face. Imagine, for a moment, how this hapless fellow must have felt—literally, like a bull in a china shop! She soothed him right away and said, "These things happen." Her phrase took the "fault" away from the customer and placed it somewhere in the world of unavoidable occurrences.

How to Be Supportive of Customers

Here are the six principles that we can use with customers to create a supportive relationship and a positive environment in which to buy. They are (1) Description, (2) Solution Focus, (3) Spontaneity, (4) Empathy, (5) Equality, and (6) Flexibility.

The Starbucks rep *described* the bags that she could use on behalf of the customer. She seemed *flexible* inasmuch as she provided him with various options from which to choose. She also seemed *solution focused*, as she sent a continuous signal that he would get exactly what he needed.

At the Franklin Mint the customer was treated to *empathy, equality,* and *flexibility*. The Assistant Manager immediately sensed how embarrassed the customer was after he broke the plates. Her first words were "Don't worry." That shows that she knew a person in his position would be apt to worry, and she wanted to prevent that from happening. By saying "These things happen," implicitly she was saying, "This could have happened to me" (*empathy*), and this shows *equality*. By giving him the option to look around to buy something he personally liked, she was demonstrating *flexibility*. In other words, "If you want to buy something, buy something you like, okay?"

Between them, these "crisis managers" manifested all the supportive communication virtues. They showed themselves to be exceptionally good conflict managers.

Try to Avoid Using Defensive Messages

Each of these scenes could have been a lot uglier if *defensive communicators* had been at work. There are six defensive messages. They include (1) Evaluation, (2) Control, (3) Strategy, (4) Neutrality, (5) Superiority, and (6) Certainty.

In the hands of a less delicate rep, the Franklin Mint scene could have been a huge public relations blunder. I can just imagine hearing a clerk say to the clumsy fellow: "Nice move!" or "Don't go into a china shop!" Or, an accusative environment could have been created if the rep boldly walked up to the fellow and demanded, "What happened here?" Each of these messages would have sounded like *negative evaluations*. Guess what we do when we think we're being wrongly or unfairly criticized?

We attack back. The fellow could have responded: "Well, the plates were loose, anyway!" or "I hardly touched them!" implying that the debacle wasn't his fault. Then, the clerk could have tried to press the point, sounding *certain that the customer was at fault*. Then, an accusation/counteraccusation defensive cycle could have been set into motion. Not only would this have alienated the butter-fingered customer, but it would have created sympathy for him among those of us who witnessed the scene. So, the store's business and goodwill may have been jeopardized, as well.

In the Starbucks situation, the manager could have dramatically worsened the outcome if she hadn't controlled her negative perceptions of the demanding customer. She might have pulled rank by stating:

I'm the manager. . . . Now, what did you say you wanted?

First of all, this intrusion would have alienated her associate, who could have felt that the manager didn't have confidence in her to handle the situation. By saying she was the manager, she'd be using a defensive message based on superiority. By injecting herself into the situation, she would have also seemed to be unduly controlling, which also arouses defensive feelings. She would have sounded strategic by forcing the customer to re-explain what he wanted. And by making him re-explain his request, she would have seemed neutral, or indifferent to the value of his time.

Exercise: A Sampler of Defensive Phrases. Here are some common phrases that can easily arouse defensiveness in customers and, therefore, jeopardize their patronage. Can you identify which of the six defensive messages matches each of these phrases? This exercise will heighten your sensitivity to the effect language can have on customers.

Remember: The six defensive messages include Evaluation, Control, Strategy, Neutrality, Superiority, and Certainty.

You'll have to . . .

You must . . .

I/We can't do this . . .

That's not possible . . .

There's no way . . .

It's not my job to . . .

It's not my fault . . .

Why can't you . . .

Don't use that language with me . . .

It's against our policy . . .

We've invested a good amount of time explaining the *empathy/supportiveness* factor because it is so significant in creating good customer relations. Now we'll turn to another significant communication factor, Listening/Active Listening.

17. "WE UNDERSTAND THE IMPORTANCE OF GOOD LISTENING"

A few years ago, one of my clients, the forerunner of Unisys Corporation, made a big splash by keying its advertising to the slogan, "We understand the importance of good listening." This campaign was so powerful in its appeal that other companies called in to beg for training in listening skills.

Human beings have a deep need to be paid attention to—to be acknowledged. By really listening to customers, we tell them that they matter and that their ideas and feelings are important. Generally, we sense that someone hasn't listened to us if she forces us to repeat ourselves. By the same token, we feel that we have been fully heard and understood when CSRs use active listening.

Active listening can be defined as the process of repeating to another person what we think he meant. For example, I was speaking to someone who donated a tremendous amount of time and effort to a school. Her work directly resulted in achieving a gift for the school in the amount of $35,000. This was easily one of the largest donations the school had ever received, but the volunteer who arranged it was hardly thanked at all for her mighty efforts.

After hearing her story, I replied:

"So, do your feel your effort wasn't appreciated?"

She shot back, "Exactly!"

I used active listening by repeating what I believed the meaning of her story to be. It was a summary—and, importantly, it was a nonjudgmental summary. I didn't say, "You're overreacting if you feel your effort wasn't appreciated," or "It's a waste to feel that your effort wasn't appreciated." I simply mirrored the meaning of what she said, and her acknowledgment of my statement told me that I was right on track.

The effective CSR will use active listening for a number of reasons.

1. It shows the customer that he was heard and understood. By itself, this relieves tension and induces cooperation.

2. It provides the customer a chance to straighten us out if we misinterpreted what we heard. The school volunteer could have replied: "No, Gary, that's not it. It's not a matter of appreciation. It's more like my work wasn't respected."

3. It gives the CSR confidence that she won't be rushing off to solve the wrong problem, which occurs quite often when we haven't listened carefully.

If people aren't listening, it's useless to talk. So, we are vitally concerned with assuring that reps hear what there is to hear and respond appropriately.

18. EVOKING THE RIGHT RESPONSES

It's certainly important to identify how reps need to communicate to be effective. But we'd be remiss if we didn't repeat here the three responses that a capable rep will evoke from customers. You'll recall from Chapter 1 that these involve the customer's *tone, gratitude,* and *recommitment.*

Tone applies to whether the customer "sings" (uses raised voice pitch) as our conversation closes. If he does, it indicates that he is happy with his encounter with the rep.

Gratitude applies to the magnitude of a customer's expression of thanks. For instance, if she simply says, "Well, thanks. Bye" this is much less intense than if she says, "Thanks so much! I really appreciate it. Bye."

Recommitment, as you know, is the customer's pledge to keep doing business with the CSR's firm. If a client says, "Well, I'll see you at your next sale!" this would certainly be a recommitment.

In this chapter we have defined the eighteen key factors that make customer contacts succeed or fail. They include:

- *General Demeanor/Cheerfulness*
- *Courtesy*
- *Articulation*
- *Speed*
- *Pitch*
- *Volume*
- *Calibration*
- *Vocabulary*
- *Grammar*
- *Energy*
- *Quickness*
- *Accuracy*
- *Appropriateness/Relevance*
- *Organization*
- *Transitions*
- *Empathy/Supportiveness*
- *Listening/Active Listening*
- *Evoking the Right Responses*

In the next chapter we explore how customer service contacts can be effectively monitored. Our discussion includes coverage of key legal requirements for workplace monitoring, including the taping and monitoring of phone calls. Monitoring by observation and practical and motivational issues will also be explored, as well as monitoring environmental factors, such as the "mood" of a service center. You'll get an opportunity to see how we monitor with TEAMeasures™ (Telephone Effectiveness Assessment Measures™). We'll also discuss the strengths and weaknesses of other monitoring methods that are currently in use.

Monitoring Customer Service

Generally, people want to be independent. Many of us would love to be able to choose what to do, when to do it, and how well to do it. In short, we'd be delighted to labor away while being left blissfully alone. But, as management guru Peter F. Drucker has pointed out, we aren't paid to do only what we like. We're paid to do what is effective for our organizations and for our customers. Monitoring tells managers whether jobs are being done correctly.

Unfortunately, there is no completely unobtrusive method of monitoring service quality. We, as managers, simply must get involved in the transaction-to-transaction details of our reps' work to accurately evaluate their performances and to assure that they receive appropriate feedback and just rewards.

For the most part, managers and their reps are only vaguely aware of how well they're doing on the job and how they've performed during specific service transactions. After customer service reps (CSRs) are trained, it's highly unusual for them to be critiqued with any regularity or accuracy. This means that they could do extremely well and have their wonderful work go unrecognized. It also means that they could be doing better in areas that are being ignored to the detriment of the company and its customers.

It's clear that customers are becoming more sophisticated and more demanding. Competition is growing more severe. Therefore, we should carefully track how our people are doing—especially the ones who have the most frequent contacts with customers. As one trainer pointed out: "If we're going to Expect, we should make sure to Inspect."

This chapter will provide you with tips for monitoring service transactions—that is, conducting meaningful service "inspections."

FIVE REASONS TO CLOSELY MONITOR CSR PERFORMANCE

There are five reasons for adopting a formal monitoring program, and they all have to do with lack of managerial attention.

1. When left to their own devices, CSRs will "erode" in their capabilities. They need to be observed, so you can give them constructive feedback. Without it, they'll lapse into a number of ineffective behaviors and generally be unaware that they're no longer on-course. Reps who aren't supervised closely may be clueless as to what they're saying, how they're saying it, and when they're saying it. Explicit feedback helps them to learn to control their communication practices.

2. If reps are "left out on the frontier" long enough, without guidance or feedback, they'll probably adopt a hodgepodge of habits that will be difficult to modify. They also run the risk of losing perspective on their relationships with customers. For example, they could grow too chummy with clients, which might prevent them from enforcing the company's rules or procedures. Or, they might move in the other direction and become callous and insensitive to the needs of clients. They might overidentify with the company, thinking it's their money that they're refunding, crediting, or otherwise managing.

3. When it comes time to compensate reps, what relevant data will we have at hand to discuss unless we've been diligently observing their work? Our evaluations should be based on real, observable events. Reps deserve fair and accurate appraisals, as does the company, and we don't want to shoot from the hip or rely on guesswork when we can access accurate information and verifiable events.

4. Morale will suffer if reps think we don't care enough to pay attention to them. When we do take notice of them, their attitudes will improve.

   Case in Point: The landmark Hawthorne Studies of several decades ago determined that productivity improves when workers believe they are important enough to warrant management attention. Morale will generally improve as long as they, or their delegates, are present in the workroom.

Try This Experiment: Without telling anyone what you're doing, take a tally of your reps' current performances. How many calls are they handling per hour, and what is the average call length? Write down these figures, because they'll become a baseline for measuring any changes that occur later.

Next, start spending more time in the service center. Just hang out, nothing more. Determine the amount of additional time you spent there. Then, remeasure your reps' performances and compare the current figures to your baseline.

Ask yourself these questions:

a. Are reps handling more calls per hour?

b. Are their calls shorter, on average?

c. Do reps seem to enjoy the additional attention they're getting? Although reps may take on a "What are you doing here?" attitude at first, they perform better as a result of feeling that they're receiving more attention. This is known as the Hawthorne Effect.

5. The fifth reason we should adopt a formal program of monitoring is that it enables us to recognize irregularities quickly and to take appropriate action, before things get out of hand.

Example: Trudy has been a capable employee of Acme Widgets for ten years. Her performance and tenure on the job earned her "Senior CSR" status and steady increases in pay. Recently, a consultant was brought in to evaluate the performance of the CSR team. He noticed that Trudy, and others, ended calls abruptly, thus seeming rude and insensitive. When her manager tried to get Trudy and the CSRs to adopt a smoother ending to calls, the group resisted, saying "This is the way we've always done it!" Because the team had developed a long-term communications pattern, Trudy had a difficult time convincing them of the need to change their phone manner.

Had Trudy been more of a continuous presence in the workroom, could she have nipped bad habits in the bud, before they had become widely adopted as part of the "informal script" of the entire group? What would you have done differently?

HOW CURRENT MONITORING PRACTICES FAIL

Many managers who attempt to monitor do so in a superficial manner, which doesn't give them an accurate record of how their people are doing. For instance, they might monitor only "extremes" in rep behavior or in service outcomes. They'll pay close attention to complimentary or complaint letters that are sent in by customers. If, for example, Trudy receives a complimentary letter from a pleased customer, the letter may be placed in her personnel file as an example of her fine work. Thus an inference, typical in such circumstances, will be made that customers, as a general rule, don't write letters unless they are really impressed. So, based on each letter, we assume that there are dozens or even hundreds of clients who feel the same way about Trudy's work but don't have the time to write a note.

The same logic may be applied to each negative letter. Managers infer that there are legions of folks who are upset, or worse, and who are leaving the fold and doing business with more agreeable competitors.

This superficial approach can be called *monitoring-by-exception.* It focuses on infrequent events and exceptional customer reactions. By examining only these events and reactions, how can managers develop an accurate understanding of how a rep is performing across the great majority of her transactions?

Monitoring-by-exception is obviously a flawed approach, for several reasons. First, such letters may not be representative at all of the results a rep produces with customers. She could have been lucky or unlucky in drawing a client who was in a good or bad mood, or one who was an avid letter-writer. Or, worse, the rep could have requested the letter of praise. Savvy CSRs will have this conversation with their favorite customers:

"Gee, I really appreciate your help, Shirley! Thanks so much."

"Well, Ms. Smith, if you feel that way, could you please take a minute to write a note to me, saying as much? I know my manager will be thrilled."

"Sure, I'll be happy to! What address should I send it to?"

If letters are disproportionately weighted in the monitoring or rep evaluation process, you can see how an ambitious or an aggressive rep can tilt the scales in his or her favor. (In another sense, I'm not so sure it's a bad thing to solicit positive letters in this manner. By writing a note, a customer will be "re-selling" herself on the value of the service she has been receiving from the rep and from the company. So, this could actually anchor her to doing business with you!)

Monitoring extremes in results also falls short in another respect. Managers seldom discover what reps did, specifically, to arouse such strong reactions. For instance, a client might praise Bill for being "helpful," but this term tells us nothing about what Bill actually did to earn the praise.

Likewise, Trudy could have sounded "rude," according to the angry letter sent by a customer. How, specifically, did she upset the person? Was it something she said? Something she didn't say or do? Or, could it have been her tone of voice?

Unfortunately, most customers are not customer service experts, so they don't have an appropriate vocabulary for analyzing their interactions with reps. So, we can't depend on them to assess in precise terms what actually transpired.

The following case illustrates this point well. It shows that numerous variables can affect a rep's performance, as well as a customer's reaction to the rep.

Communication Case #1: It's 9:05 on Monday morning. Bill sits down to work, fidgeting in his chair, which always seems to throw out his lower back. He logs onto the computer, takes a sip of chilly coffee from his defective thermos, and groans, mostly under his breath, "Well, here goes another day." No one hears exactly what he said, but Shirley, Bill's supervisor, thought she heard something coming from Bill's direction, and asked:

"What did you say, Bill?"

"Oh, nothing. How're you doing Shirley?"

"I'm okay. How 'bout you?"

"Sure, fine."

"Really?

"Yeah, I said I was okay, didn't I?"

"Yes, but I just got the feeling that something was wrong."

"Did I *say* anything was wrong?" Bill rattled back.

"No, but . . . Well, forget I said anything."

"Okay by me!" Bill retorted.

Turning to her ringing phone, Shirley answered it and announced her name. When she asked, "How may I help you?" the customer seemed to take offense.

"Well, I don't know if you can help me, and judging from how you sound, I tend to doubt it."

"How about giving me a try?" Shirley asked, summoning all the cheerfulness she could.

"There you go again!" snapped the customer.

"There I go again, what?" Shirley asked, dazed by the comment.

"With that tone of voice."

"What tone? Is this some kind of put-on or something?"

The customer's voice grew louder: "You sound very short and impatient with me, young lady, and I simply won't take that from someone whose salary I'm paying!"

"Look, I'm just trying to do my job, and you're jumping on me for nothing, and furthermore, *you don't pay my salary, my company does.*"

"I want a supervisor!"

"I am a supervisor!"

"Well, then, I want your superior—now! Get him on the line."

"First of all, my supervisor is a she, not a he, and second, you have no right to boss me around, but please hold and I'll see if she's available!"

And with those words, Shirley placed the customer on hold and stared at the phone, hoping it would catch fire. She found herself struggling for breath and feeling uncharacteristically immobilized by this turn of events.

Bill was speechless, yet his mouth looked as if it were forming a large letter "O." He had never known Shirley to have such a short fuse. Fumbling for words, he timidly asked:

"What's, uh, going on, Shirley?"

"Well, I've got this complete idiot on hold, and he can just stay there awhile to cool his heels."

Bill probed further. "What does he want?"

"To speak to *my* supervisor. That's a laugh."

"Want me to talk to him?" Bill asks with a grin.

"Since when are you my supervisor?"

"You know," Bill resumes, "maybe I can calm him down and get things back on track. Worth a try, right?"

"No, I want to handle this myself," Shirley asserted.

"Don't say I didn't ask," Bill warned.

Leaning forward like a panther, Shirley slowly asked, "Now, what do you mean by *that*, Bill?"

"Nothing Shirley, nothing." Sensing Shirley was about to lose it, Bill added quickly, "Look, I'm just going back to my work now, okay, Shirley?"

Curling her lip like Clint Eastwood, Shirley whispered, "You . . . just . . . do . . . that . . . , Bill." While this was going on, the customer got disconnected.

On Wednesday, an overnight letter arrived, addressed to the president of the company. The return address bore the name of the angry customer and the envelope was marked "Urgent."

Discussion Questions

1. If you were the customer, what would you have said in your letter to the president?

2. Imagine being in Shirley's shoes. How would she explain her interaction with the customer? What would Bill say?

3. From a communications perspective, how would you explain what you saw and heard? In other words, what really went on here?

If the president had only the letter to go on, would he or she have an accurate and complete description of the events that provoked it? Probably not. So, when monitoring rep performance, you can see how dangerous it can be to attribute too much importance to letters.

PLUSES AND MINUSES OF CUSTOMER SURVEYS

Some companies attempt to monitor performance through questionnaires and surveys. By tapping into a cross-section of customers, surveys can avoid some of the flaws of managing extremes.

Instead of making inferences about customer satisfaction from only a few data points, such as letters, a survey receives input from a significant number of people. Emphasis is placed on assigning numerical values to responses, so a statistical portrait of client reactions is achieved.

Current survey results can be compared to previous surveys, from in-house as well as outside the industry. Managers can get a sense as to how effective their people are relative to their own past efforts, as well as to a larger peer group of CSRs from other companies.

However, surveys can have drawbacks. They may take considerable time to construct, to deliver to customers, to be returned, and to tally and interpret. If we mail out a survey today, the earliest we can expect results to be returned is within a week. Most of our returns will arrive two to three weeks later. And some people won't return their questionnaires for many weeks, if at all. By the time we have tallied and interpreted surveys, they may no longer represent the reality of many clients, or of the marketplace. Thus surveys must be carefully designed and implemented to ensure timely and accurate results.

Example: Before some recent stock market volatility, I was exceedingly happy with the performance of my discount brokerage company. I was able to get quotes quickly by phone and execute trades superfast via computer. But my satisfaction changed, radically, on the morning the market "crashed." Instead of being able to get immediate stock quotes by phone, I found the access number was constantly busy!

So, my fortunes were plummeting before my eyes, and I was helpless. I felt really letdown and not nearly as "bullish" on my broker. An instant before the crash, my impression was nothing but positive. A day later, it was in the pits, along with some of my financial holdings.

This experience highlights another, significant problem of using surveys: *Unless they are carefully designed, they may not really measure what we think they're measuring.* As long as the stock market kept rising, and my wealth increased, I was at peace with the world and with all my vendors—brokers included. But when that rosy scenario changed, my satisfaction changed as well.

My impressions of my broker, unfortunately, are tied to my impressions of how well I'm doing financially. If things aren't good, I'm probably going to spread the blame around and implicate my broker, even if that firm makes no specific investment recommendations.

Regrettably, it's simply human nature to overreact this way.

Surveys are also problematic because certain clusters of respondents will be overrepresented in the group of returned questionnaires. Respondents who are at the extremes, whether happy or unhappy, will be inclined to return the documents, whereas those in the middle will not. So, this skews the results, thus making it difficult for managers to make appropriate inferences from the documents that are returned.

The "garbage in/garbage out" principle can also be a problem. If you're lucky, you'll get responses appropriate to the questions you ask, assuming the survey has been properly designed and the customers understand what you're trying to get at. But what if you ask the wrong questions? Or, what if your questions don't really tap into what customers want? What then?

For example, some time ago, Coca-Cola customers were given taste-tests of something that the company called "New Coke." They were queried about their impressions of the drink, and they liked it. On the strength of these results, the company replaced its traditional Coke formula with New Coke. The market rebelled. Protests were made, and the company revived its former brand by calling it Classic Coke. What happened?

Those who were surveyed weren't asked whether they would support the replacement of Coke with New Coke. They were asked only if they liked the new concoction.

The lesson is clear: If they are not properly designed and implemented, tidy and neatly tallied questionnaires may not give you any meaningful guidance.

Example: Some customer service surveys ask these questions:

1. Was the representative polite at all times?
2. Did the representative seem knowledgeable?
3. Was the representative helpful?

"Polite" and "knowledgeable" and "helpful" can mean different things to different customers. Moreover, these words may not be relevant descriptors of the conversations customers had with reps.

Let's say a customer called to ask for a mutual fund quotation. How impolite, unhelpful, or ignorant can a rep be in that sort of brief call? Even if the rep was flawed in her treatment of the customers, they may be reluctant "to get her into trouble" by being utterly frank when answering survey questions. In research, this is referred to as an experimenter effect. When people know they're being observed, or that their reactions are being measured, they tend to distort their opinions. This may take the form of trying to give the experimenter what the client thinks he wants, with regard to a response. In other words, folks can try to behave like "good customers" and thus express only their most congenial feelings. They're being "nice" instead of completely honest.

Of course, surveys are largely descriptive. They'll tell you how some customers say they think and feel. But their biggest shortcoming is that they won't tell you what variables your reps can change to improve customer perceptions.

When we discuss TEAMeasures (Telephone Effectiveness Assessment Measures), which we mentioned in the previous chapter, you'll be shown a device not only for quantifying customer responses but for telling reps, explicitly, what they need to change, to get consistently better results.

A TRIED AND TRUE MONITORING DEVICE: MANAGING BY "WALKING AROUND"

A good way to monitor work is by using the technique known as *managing by walking around* (*MBWA*). MBWA was discussed at length in the business best-seller *In Search of Excellence*, published a number of years ago. The theory supporting MBWA is that managers need to mind the store, and a good way to do so is by actively *patrolling* it. This is especially important in managing phone centers, where there are exceedingly high customer transaction volumes. During an hour in many call centers, CSRs can field twenty calls or more.

So, in a phone center, if a rep is out-of-sorts or in a bad mood, he can do tremendous damage. If managers aren't within earshot, they'll be clueless when it comes to knowing and correcting what's going on. And a bad attitude or performance that starts with a single rep can quickly contaminate the entire work group. Like a virus, a mood swing can spread very quickly and infect your entire staff.

The following true story illustrates how one rep can affect an entire group.

Communication Case #2: The Bud Story. Bud, one of your most experienced reps, seems unusually quiet. This has been going on for several weeks, yet it hasn't affected his production. You're concerned that he's having a negative effect on his work group, because new people seem to crawl into their own defensive shells and stay there. Their production is below normal.

What's going on here, and what are you prepared to do about it?

This is a part of a case study that I discuss in my seminar, Monitoring, Measuring, and Managing Customer Service. It presents the customer service manager with a real problem. How can you manage this situation? Usually, the first thing I hear is that Bud "has a bad attitude." This may be true, but his attitude isn't affecting his own performance. So, what can you do about it?

Almost everyone agrees that we should sit down with Bud and talk it through. But, in the seminar, when we role-play this meeting, nothing seems to get resolved. Bud says he's fine and that you're imagining things. Anyway, are you really trying to link his attitude to the inadequate performance of your new recruits? That doesn't seem fair to Bud. How defensible is this position?

This case, based on a real situation that I faced as a new manager, repeats itself every day in countless companies. Unfortunately, most managers make a classical error. They try to improve Bud's attitude and to manage his personality. They would be better served by examining his actual behavior, as we shall discuss.

Attitudes Versus Behaviors: What Are We Really After?

According to researchers, attitudes have three components: (1) cognitive, or what we know about something; (2) affective, or how we feel about something; and (3) conative, or how we behave toward a situation. Managers err by trying to control components (1) and (2). Generally, this is frustrating and fruitless. Managers intrude into a dangerous area when they try to play "amateur psychologist" with their people. My advice: Don't try to change how people think—simply concentrate on how they behave.

There's Nothing Quite Like Being There, in the Room

The Bud Story reinforces the point made previously: Managers should be in the workroom frequently enough to witness what's going on. If Bud is doing something counterproductive, he can be asked about it, on the spot. And if his behaviors are truly outrageous, the manager will have "the smoking gun" in terms of evidence that she can bring into disciplinary meetings. *Being able to say "I saw Bud do X" is a lot more appropriate than to say "I believe Bud was doing X."*

How can managers assure that they'll have enough time to personally monitor reps reasonably frequently? That's easy to answer. Make sure that there is at least one "manager's desk" in the work center, placed in the middle of the room. This way, the manager can hear what is being said in every direction. In large centers, you may want to have several managers' desks strategically located. Each manager should bring some paperwork to the desk. That way, he or she will be doing more than just waiting for something to happen.

Use Praise as Well as Criticism

You might feel self-conscious if you believe that you're in the workroom only for the purpose of catching people doing the wrong things. Please remember that you're there to reinforce and to praise the right practices, as well. As you'll see later on when we discuss SEAmeasures (Supervisor Effectiveness Assessment Measures), you should strive to balance your criticism with positive and helpful points. That way, your presence will be constructive and you'll be taken seriously, but you'll also be "easy to take."

But What If You Don't Feel Comfortable Being in the Workroom?

If you don't feel comfortable patrolling the workroom, then you should practice the behavior of MBWA. The more time you spend in the room, the more comfortable you'll become. It's important to develop this sense of comfort.

There is no substitute for your physical presence. You need to directly perceive what's going on, to gauge your group's abilities, and to assess your options for developing them. Remember that your reps should never feel so at-home in their workspaces as to believe that they completely own them and that your presence is the equivalent of "trespassing." Any nervousness, or "fish out of water" feeling you experience will signal insecurity to your associates, and this will destabilize your role as a part of the management team.

Here is an exercise to help you develop a sense of comfort as a manager.

Exercise: Patrolling the Workroom. Plan to spend at least ten minutes each morning and ten minutes each afternoon in the room. Vary the times, so you won't be expected.

Walk around, and say hello to each rep as you pass by. Try to smile as much as you can, to send a signal that you're comfortable with what you're seeing and hearing. Go slowly enough to hear several seconds of each phone conversation. Make a mental note of the pluses and minuses of how your folks are treating customers.

Your job right now is not to offer criticism or tips, unless you sense you must for the good of the company. All you want to do is gradually become more of a presence in the center. After you complete this task, ask yourself these questions:

1. Which reps are happy to see me?

2. Which reps aren't happy to see me, and why not?

3. How are my supervisors responding to my presence? Are they nervous, or turf-protective?

4. What's the best "performance" I overheard as I patrolled?

5. And the worst?

6. How did I feel?

7. How did I behave? Comfortably? Uptight?

8. What did I learn by patrolling that I would have never learned by sitting in my office?

If you can't answer all these questions right away, don't worry about it. You'll become much more proficient and "present" and less self-conscious as you repeat your patrolling exercises.

Before we leave this topic, I should point out that patrolling should be done in all customer service situations. Managers need to know, firsthand, what is happening on the front lines. For example, how often have you gone into a restaurant where the manager visited your table and asked "How is everything?" They're supposed to do this, as a quality-control measure, to make sure the kitchen staff and waiters are on their game. If they're not, it's usually an easy thing for the manager to correct in a timely fashion. What the boss doesn't want is a disgruntled patron suffering in silence and deciding to never come into the place again.

When I was taking a class on the subject of franchising, the professor pointed out: "If you're not comfortable walking up to patrons and asking, 'How is everything?' then you don't belong in the restaurant business." As you can guess, I'd extend that maxim to all customer service settings.

SHOULD YOU ADOPT AN EXPLICIT "CODE OF BEHAVIOR" FOR YOUR WORK GROUP?

Customer service centers can be very moody organisms. Slam a phone, raise your voice, or make a nasty comment about a peer, a manager, or a customer, and you'll change the temper of the place in a nanosecond. Productivity can tank or it can soar depending on mood swings, which can warm a place like a sunrise or devastate it like a tornado.

Managers need to control moods as much as they pay attention to any feature of customer service work. It does no good to legislate happiness, but we can set forth clear behavioral boundaries in which associates should operate.

Here are some elements that you might want to consider including in a behavioral code.

1. We will speak only well of customers. This discourages the negative practice of ending a conversation and blurting out, "That customer is such an idiot!" When reps involve themselves in critique sessions about customers, they take their attention away from the call to come. Moreover, how can one spew venom one second and a second later speak "honey" to the next customer? Verbal poison contaminates calls, and its influence kills attitudes and injures performance.

2. We will speak only well of company associates. This reduces backbiting and discourages feuding and cliques.

3. We will refrain from phone slamming, desk pounding, and making any loud or offensive noises or distractions that can negatively affect our associates' effectiveness. This says we have a responsibility to maintain a problem-free atmosphere and that our nonverbal behavior affects others.

4. We will not complain to our associates about compensation, work methods, tasks, or responsibilities. When we have complaints, we will share them with managers as quickly as we can, in a setting conducive to their proper consideration.

5. We will offer help to associates in need, and we will turn to associates and to managers when we are in need of assistance.

Such a code creates ground rules for your team to follow. It also provides managers with explicit tools for controlling moods in the phone center. The complainer, or informal leader who has a gripe with management, who takes a problem out on his associates can be reprimanded and be properly sanctioned. Without a code of behavior, we might try to co-exist with negativity. Top customer service results can't be sustained in an atmosphere that permits negative communications.

Look at the preceding code. What behaviors would you add or delete from this list?

SHOULD YOU MONITOR AND ENFORCE DRESS CODES?

Designers tell us that we're becoming a less formal culture and that our clothing preferences reflect this attitude. They're saying that "dressing-down" is becoming a national trend. Necktie-optional workplaces for men are becoming more common in places far from California and Hawaii, pioneers of casual living.

Phone centers have been fashion renegades for decades. Kelly-Springfield Tire Company used to house its telemarketers in a separate building where they could wear what they wanted and not upset the rank and file.

Many industries began without dress codes and have struggled to stay that way. Software firms often cut a lot of slack for developers and for those in tech support and customer service who don't see customers on a day-to-day basis. (I recall being able to consult to one software company while I was dressed in jeans, boots, and a sports shirt. My client was located at the beach, so it was an unwritten perk of the job for people to feel a part of the lifestyle beyond its doors.)

Nonetheless, dress codes have their advocates. "People should be reminded they're at work," a manager from Honda declared when the subject came up in one of my recent Customer Service Management seminars. Supporters of this view maintain that formal business attire gets people into the mood to work and reinforces their feeling of professionalism. They seem more serious about their work.

And if even they're on the phone, some managers claim reps sound better if they are dressed well: crisp, prepared, disciplined, if you will.

Of course, requiring formal business attire can cost workers a substantial amount of money. When wardrobe purchases and dry cleaning are calculated, it can run into thousands of dollars per year.

Being free from conforming to a dress code can be a form of comfort-compensation for some workers. It gives them "psychic income" that may induce them to stick around longer than they would otherwise. Others say they don't really feel they're employed unless there are clear reminders of this fact, such as those supplied by uniforms.

Determining whether to adopt a restrictive dress code in a phone center is a tough decision. Changing an existing clothing policy can be even tougher. A manager at Time/Life who was new to the company burst on the casual scene and announced that henceforth suits and ties for men, and skirts for women, were required. Within a few weeks, 50% of the phone workers quit.

So, devising or enforcing a dress code should be much more than a casual decision. And you need to ask yourself if you're willing to monitor clothing choices and serve as a "fashion cop."

TRY USING "DIRECT POINTING" TO HELP YOUR REPS

One of the keys to managing effectively is making sure that managers are speaking the same language reps are speaking about communication events. This is almost impossible unless we do one of two things: (1) We carefully define our terms; or (2) We directly point to what we're referring to.

I'll cover definitions of terms at considerable length in a later chapter on customer service measurement. For now, let's look at the second way of making sure we're on the same page with reps, the technique known as *direct pointing*.

The other day I was watching my daughter play soccer, when another Dad called out my name, pointed to the sky, and said, "Look!" Immediately, I saw a huge jet stream in the sky, something that could have been made by an asteroid or a missile. If he hadn't pointed to this event, I would have missed it.

I'm sure I saw something similar to what he saw, even allowing for differences in our visual acuity and our respective vantage points on the field. That's about as clearly and concretely as two human beings can communicate. We had almost the exact same perceptual experience at the same time.

However, once things are put into words, we move up the "ladder of abstraction," as linguists say. And our chances of misunderstandings, when we aren't really seeing things from the same viewpoint, increase dramatically. By directly pointing to the phenomenon, my friend used a better medium than language to convey something to me quickly and accurately.

We can't interrupt service situations to identify what reps are doing right and what they are doing wrong. But, as you'll see in the next section, we can record transactions. This will assist us in directly pointing out strengths and weaknesses.

IF YOU'RE GOING TO MONITOR, YOU SHOULD CREATE AN OBJECTIVE RECORD

Can you imagine being the coach of a modern football team and deciding not to use videotapes of your games and those of your competitors? That would be preposterous, because, as the saying goes, pictures are worth thousands of words. With video, for example, a coach can freeze the frame and say, "See! That's where you missed the tackle." The video provides an objective record of what occurred. But how can we create objective records of what occurs during customer service transactions? One way is to tape telephone transactions. Tapes don't exaggerate or downplay what occurs, as people may inadvertently do. They dispassionately replay what took place, and this helps us to be objective managers.

When you have an audiotape of conversations, you can monitor several things: (1) Is the rep on or off the language of the Call Path? (2) Is he using the appropriate vocal tones to support the text? (3) Is he employing the correct timing to bring the text to life? (4) And, finally, is the customer reacting positively or negatively?

You'll find that most problems can be diagnosed by answering the first three questions. Naturally, if the rep isn't using the exact text of the Call Path, it can't work its magic on customers, right? Most often, the rep will think she's using it correctly, when in fact she has strayed far off the path. By playing a tape of calls, she can hear proof that she's not on the program. When calls are taped, especially after the Call Path has been introduced, we can clarify what is really going on within the "world of the call." This, after all is said and done, is what the customer really hears and how the customer really reacts.

LEGAL ISSUES IN THE TAPING OF CONVERSATIONS

In this section, we'll explore the nature of the laws dealing with the monitoring and taping of telephone conversations. As a general rule, the nonconsensual or secret monitoring or taping of calls is prohibited. Under U.S. Federal Law, this means that the manager who listens in on, or records, a conversation without the consent of at least one of the parties to the call is committing a crime. Nonconsensual monitoring or taping of calls is also illegal under the statutes of at least 13 states. California's Penal Code Section 632, known as the Invasion of Privacy Statute, is typical of current state restrictions. It makes it a crime to monitor or record the conversations of people without the consent of all parties. Penalties include a $2,500 fine and a year in county jail or state prison. This can be filed either as a misdemeanor or as a felony. Repeat offenders are faced with even stiffer penalties.

Misconceptions About the Law

There are many misconceptions about the circumstances under which one may or may not monitor or record calls. Following are examples of misconceptions and their implications.

1. **Some managers foster the belief that "if the monitoring or taping is done for training purposes only, it's okay."** Not true. Section 632 is not a specific-intent crime, which means your frame of mind is irrelevant. By analogy, if you're caught doing 85 in a 45-mile zone, your lack of intent to speed is of no concern to the officer who tickets you.

2. **Many people confuse "notice" with "consent."** They think it's okay to intrude on calls if people know what's going on. Big mistake. Lots of banks and other large firms announce at the beginning of calls that callers might be monitored or be taped. This notification falls short of obtaining someone's voluntary permission for the intrusion. Consent means notice plus voluntary approval.

3. **Some folks think that you can simply have an electronic "beep-tone" chime into the conversation every so many seconds and that this will enable you to monitor or tape legally.** Most customers have no idea what the beep means, so we may not even achieve "notice," let alone consent.

4. **Some managers say: "It's no big deal to break the law because it's seldom enforced."** Not true. Prosecutions under Section 632 have occurred; even if there had not been any prosecutions so far, would you like to be the first one?

5. **"The penalties, even if you're tried and convicted, are minimal."** This is a huge misconception. How many calls are monitored or taped in a single day? Firms that tape all their calls through a centralized switch could be guilty of committing hundreds of punishable offenses every day. How much is 100 times $2,500 and 100 times one year in prison? Get the picture? Every call can constitute an offense.

6. **"No one would want to prosecute us—we're pillars of the community."** Your firm could be saintly but still get into trouble. Numerous prosecutors, attorneys general, and city attorneys are politicians. They need popular issues with which to get elected and re-elected. Attacking companies that seem to be wiretapping or eavesdropping could be very appealing, especially in an era in which citizens are alarmed over diminution of privacy.

7. "If one law says it's okay to tape or monitor, then it's always okay." Lawyers will tell you that on a given day it's very difficult to discover what "The Law" is, because there are numerous laws and sources of law that govern our conduct. For instance, the Federal Communications Commission (FCC), which has some authority over phone conversations, is concerned only about one-party consent to monitor or tape calls. But this agency can't and won't speak for your state, which can pass a law similar to California's Invasion of Privacy Statute.

The California Public Utilities Commission may say that it's okay to monitor or tape with a beep-tone, but Penal Code Section 632 does not agree. So, by following one dictate, you could still be violating another.

8. "If my firm isn't in California or in one of the jurisdictions that requires all-party consent to monitor or tape, I'm free to do what I want." Wrong again. If you call into California, or if Californians call you, and you perform the offending activity, you can be hauled into California's courts under what are termed "long-arm" statutes.

9. "If monitoring or taping is so bad, why do firms like Radio Shack® continue to sell 'telephone pick-ups' and devices for tapping into calls?" Gun shops sell guns, but they don't pull the trigger.

10. "If our corporate counsel says it's potentially illegal, we simply won't monitor or tape calls." There is no substitute for consulting with a lawyer if you want strictly legal information. However, after reading Section 632, most practicing attorneys will probably have a knee-jerk reaction. They'll advise you to "Stop monitoring and taping." *They'll be less likely to tell you how to monitor or tape within the parameters of the law and to do so in a way that won't offend customers or employees.*

As a good manager, you may feel that listening to calls is the best way to lead your people to higher levels of achievement. This could put you into a bind. If you do what you feel is right as a manager, then you could be a criminal; and if you don't monitor or tape, you could be an irresponsible manager. So, how can you tape calls legally?

How to Legally Gain Consent for Taping Inbound Calls

Happily, techniques exist for complying with the law and not negatively affecting your phone conversations. I have crafted scripts that enable people to obtain consent from customers, during inbound as well as outbound calls. I recommend you obtain consent on each and every call you tape or monitor, and it's very easy to do. Let's start with the inbound version of the "consent statement" for taping:

Hello, the Goodman Organization. This is Gary on a recorded line. How may I help you?

If you're thinking that this is similar to the standard greeting, you're absolutely right. The only words that have been added are "on a recorded line." Let's examine this phrase while pointing out how your reps should deliver it.

First of all, the phrase "on a recorded line" was carefully constructed. It's short and to the point. It is also a statement and not a question, so it implicitly discourages a comment from the customer after he hears this phrase. Moreover, it's supposed to sound humdrum and routine. It implies, "We're taping this call, but it's nothing to get excited about." This situation should be reinforced by the rep's tone of voice. So, when your reps come to this phrase, their tone of voice should fall. Then, when they get to "How may I help you?" the standard Call Path instructions apply. The word "you" should go way up in tone.

The phrase "on a recorded line" is sandwiched between the announcement of the rep's name and the question "How may I help you?" Being placed here, it tends to blend with the rest of the Greeting, and not bring undue attention to itself. The result is a phrase that tells the listener he is being recorded, but it accomplishes this task in a very low-key manner. Immediately after a client hears the Greeting, she can decide whether to object to the taping or to simply go along with it, without saying anything about it.

Most people will ignore it, and they'll quickly state their business or ask their question. As long as the text, tone, and timing are done properly, less than one person in five hundred will express a desire not to be taped.

Occasionally, a few customers ask, "Why are you taping?" I'll give you two simple and truthful responses that you can use. You can say:

1. "For training purposes, and how may I help you?" or

2. "For quality improvement purposes, and how may I help you?"

Usually, that'll be satisfactory, and you'll be able to return to the content of the conversation without further delay.

Gaining Customer Consent During Outbound Calls

Here's the outbound version of the consent phrase:

Hello, Mr./Ms. Jones? This is Gary Goodman with the Goodman Organization, on a recorded line—How are you doing? That's good. The reason I'm calling is ..

The same principles apply to the text, tone, and timing as apply to inbound calls. The rep should ask the listener how he is in order to provide him with immediate means to object to the recording process. If she gets someone who says "I'd rather not be taped," she should take it in stride. Respond by saying: "No problem, we won't record this call." Then promptly turn off the tape recorder and continue the conversation.

You'll Also Need the Rep's Consent

Reps also have legal rights that must be respected. So, when you hire them, have your lawyers draft a note that says something to this effect:

I consent to allowing my work activities and telephone conversations to be monitored and electronically recorded by management as a condition of accepting and continuing my employment with XYZ Corporation. If, at any time, I withhold my consent to these activities, I understand I will be subject to immediate termination or reassignment.

The Logistics of Taping Calls

When I have reps tape calls, I like to use a portable tape recorder with a telephone "pick-up," which is a wire that attaches to the handset from the recorder. I'll locate the unit at the rep's desk and plug in the recorder right there. It's then up to the rep to start the taping at the beginning of calls, and then to stop taping as calls conclude. I let the rep do it, for several reasons:

1. Reps feel that they are in charge of the process, and, in a sense, they are. By working the machine, they participate, and this creates positive interest. I also tell them I don't need any personal calls on the tape, so if any come in by accident, reps are instructed to simply stop the tape. By saying I don't need to hear personal calls on the tape, I'm sending a signal to reps that says, "Look, I'm not trying to catch you doing something you shouldn't be doing." This builds trust.

2. By controlling the recorder, reps can stop the taping right away, if a customer so requests. This capability enables us to remain in compliance with the law.

3. Reps must say "on a recorded line" only when they're actually recording. So, let's assume it's Tuesday morning, and I'm going to have two of my reps, out of a group of twenty, recording today. Eighteen people don't have to worry about using this phrase, because they're not recording. This reduces the likelihood that we'll encounter clients who will object to the taping process.

Many modern phone systems allow the automated taping of numerous calls without human intervention. These tools enable managers to tape a sampling of all rep calls or to concentrate on taping only a few reps or conversations at a time. This makes taping administratively easier, but, from a legal standpoint and a motivational standpoint, I'd rather taping be performed by the individual reps, at their workstations.

Legally, what happens if a client says she doesn't want to be taped? How can reps disable the taping process from their workstations if the mechanics of taping are remotely operated? This creates a practical problem. To prove it to yourself, perform this exercise:

Exercise: Refuse to Be Taped. Call into any high-volume phone center. You'll probably hear a recorded message as you're waiting that says, "Your call may be recorded (or monitored) to assure quality service." (If you can't think of a company to call, call The Gas Company's customer service line in Los Angeles. When the rep comes onto the line, say this: "I heard your machine say this call may be recorded. What if I don't want to be recorded?"

Stop right there. You'll hear a gasp from the rep, because he'll probably be unaware of what the recorded Greeting is saying. Then, he'll rush to get a supervisor, and you'll be tied up for many minutes, while they try to figure out what their policies are regarding taping and dealing with reluctant clients.

Ask yourself, "Do I want to force my reps and my customers to jump through the same hoops?"

Are "Monitoring" and "Taping" the Same Thing?

Saying "Your call may be monitored to assure quality service" is not the same as saying "on a recorded line." If you're monitoring, you're listening in on the conversation, as if you're holding an extension phone to your ear. If you're recording, you're making a potentially permanent electronic record of the conversation, which is a related, but different act.

So, which word should you use in your consent statement? If you're only monitoring, then say "monitoring." If you're taping, then say, "on a recorded line." But please don't say "monitoring" if you're taping. How come? The consent you get should fit the activity for which you need consent. By using the proper terms, you'll obtain the proper consent.

One more thought regarding customer consent: We aren't officially asking for their approval. In other words, we don't expect to say "on a recorded line" and hear customers respond "Oh, okay. Go ahead and do that." What we're obtaining is implied consent. Once listeners have heard what we're doing, and they've been given an immediate and reasonable opportunity to withhold consent, we assume we have obtained a proper measure of consent sufficient to comply with prevailing laws.

Of course, as with any information applying to the law, it is best to check with your corporate attorney to confirm the viability of using the approaches mentioned here, as well as to obtain the very latest changes that may have occurred in the law.

Don't Permit the "Secret" Taping or Monitoring of Calls

Aside from the legal problems you might invite, it is unwise to secretly tape or monitor calls for another significant reason. Reps hate it when they feel that managers are "trying to catch them doing something wrong." Who can blame them? Most folks experience some degree of test apprehension or performance anxiety under the best of conditions. But when we try to be stealthy in our evaluations, we only increase the stress levels of reps to unreasonable levels.

Some managers erroneously think that the only way they can get reliable data about rep achievement is by obtaining it secretly. After all, that is when employees have their "guard down," right?

There's some truth in the fact that one might be able to see reps at their "worst," but who wants to do that? Don't we want reps to do their best at all times? Furthermore, it's unlikely that a rep will be able to go from being totally hang-loose to fully complying with the Call Path simply because she is informed that monitoring or recording is about to be done. People just don't "change their stripes" that quickly.

Remember MBWA. By having a continuous presence in the room, managers can assure themselves that reps are "on the program" between formal taping or monitoring periods. By the time formal taping or monitoring is slated, reps should be in the habit of performing the Call Path the right way. Then coaching and counseling can be used to improve performance and to motivate reps to higher levels of achievement.

Secrecy of any kind tends to raise suspicions and defensiveness. Most contemporary firms want to operate openly, in a supportive atmosphere.

ULTIMATELY, WHAT WE'RE REALLY AFTER IS SELF-MONITORING

As managers, we're always going to want to monitor the work process—not just to observe what's going on but also to see the process from the rep's point of view as well as that of the customer. But what we really aspire to is creating an atmosphere in which reps are continuously performing self-monitoring. Reps shouldn't find management's evaluations a major surprise if they are continuously aware of the criteria that are used to assess the quality of their work.

To get reps to take full responsibility for their work-products, managers need to help them move through three distinct levels of motivation: (1) compliance, (2) identification, and (3) internalization.

When you start using the Call Path, your first task will be to get your reps to comply—to use it. This, as you know, may involve a struggle, and you'll be relying on your formal authority as a manager to get reps to enact this element of an improved customer service program. Compliance is the lowest level of employee motivation. If reps were asked, "Why are you doing the Call Path?" they'd probably reply, "Because management is making me do it!" Unfortunately, few reps will have the maturity or insight to immediately and willingly adopt the Call Path. But after it has been in use, its benefits should add up. Ask reps what they're hearing from customers. Be specific.

"Are your customers *singing*?"

"Are customers *thanking you profusely*?"

"Are customers *recommitting their business*?"

When you fish for these reactions, you'll hook the reps, and they will realize that the Call Path, and your Herculean efforts, *are paying off for them*. This is a critical moment, because it is at this stage that reps start to *sell themselves on the program.*

They'll then move into the second stage of motivation, which is called *identification.* They'll begin to identify with the program, because they'll see benefits in it for them. After all, it is the vehicle through which customers are singing, thanking them profusely, and recommitting.

Getting these positive results for one's efforts is a lot more enjoyable than not getting them! So, when reps start identifying their interests with the company's interests in having the Call Path performed, you will have brought them to the second level of motivation.

The third and deepest level is called *internalization.* At this stage, if you asked reps why they're using the Call Path, they would say, "Because it works, and because I enjoy it." When this level is reached, you'll need to monitor less often, because reps will be monitoring themselves. Additionally, they'll become so sensitive to customers' reactions that they'll be able to diagnose their own shortcomings. I've heard a lot of reps say, "He didn't sing as much as he could have, because I forgot to stair-step!" When reps reach the internalization point, they could easily coach and counsel other reps. It is at this point in their development that you can turn them into team leaders and supervisors.

Measuring Customer Service Representatives

How do we know when a CSR is "great" versus merely "good," "average," or "below average"? How can we feel confident in making this judgment? Moreover, what proof do we have that we have delivered first-class service to our customers?

This chapter will examine various methods of measuring customer service achievement. It will also explain the Telephone Effectiveness Assessment Measures, also known as (TEAMeasures), the instrument I have devised for evaluating customer service calls.

HOW SOME REPS ARE MEASURED

At many companies, reps are evaluated based on the number of transactions they handle, as well as the length of those transactions. These can be valid indices of performance; however, they are often used in a shallow manner, as the following example illustrates.

I was retained as a consultant by the "Sandy" Company, where the average CSR call length was about three minutes. The better reps' calls were closer to two minutes. Less competent reps were identified as those whose calls substantially exceeded the three-minute average. Reps whose calls exceeded the three-minute average justified their performances by claiming that they offered more thorough explanations to customers. Therefore, they asserted that they handled customers better than the less chatty reps.

When I interviewed the Sandy Company's reps who consistently kept their average call length to a minimum, they disclosed to me that they had learned certain "tricks" for "beating the system." For example, when a customer called and asked for five stock quotations, the system-beaters would say: "I'm sorry, but I'm allowed to give you only three quotes. You'll need to call back for the other two." Of course, this frustrated the customers, who wanted one-call satisfaction for all their questions, but it made the Average Call Length and Transaction Volume statistics of certain reps look good.

YOU'LL GET WHAT YOU MEASURE—ONE WAY OR ANOTHER

No manager wants her reps to "beat the system" in the manner just described. But if all we reward is a short, average call length, believe me, reps will find clever ways to shorten calls!

What the Sandy Company failed to do was to show reps how they could reduce call length while increasing customer satisfaction. After we introduced the techniques described in this book, including the Call Path, calls were shortened by 15–25%. Reps were grateful because they no longer had to figure out how to accomplish this feat on their own.

TEN CRITERIA FOR MEASURING CUSTOMER SERVICE CALLS

Before getting into the details of my measurement system, we should explore what I believe to be the ten attributes of any successful conversational measurement tool. If you choose to develop your own measurement system you can build from this foundation.

Any measurement system should include the following attributes.

1. *The categories of measurement should be clear.*

2. *The device should present an easy way to quantify data to establish meaningful statistical baselines.*

3. *All categories should be operationally defined.* For instance, in defining "articulation," we don't say it means being understandable to listeners. We define it as "The full formation of words, so they are immediately comprehensible to a listener of reasonable sensibilities." This tells phone reps

to form their words fully. By defining our terms operationally, we prescribe a clear course of behavior that reps can follow.

4. *The categories should be comprehensive.* All meaningful events in conversations must be captured by the measures.

5. *Each category must be isomorphic.* Categories need to mean one thing, and only one thing, and they should not intrude into another category's meaning.

6. *Measures need to be flexible, to allow interpretation of unusual telephone events.*

7. *Measures need to seem fair and reasonable to CSRs and to managers.*

8. *Measures should produce perceptual agreement among users.* This is often referred to as *inter-judge reliability.* Users with different experiential and educational backgrounds should be able to use the same measures and judge conversations the same way. Reps and managers should score the same conversations within a margin of error of no more than plus or minus 2%. For instance, on a 100-point scale, if Manager X assigns a score of 82 to a call, Manager Y's score should be no more than 84 and no less than 80.

9. *The measures should be universally applicable.* In other words, they should be tested and proven across companies and across industries.

10. *The measures should define and improve customer satisfaction with greater reliability than the methods they replace.*

TELEPHONE EFFECTIVENESS ASSESSMENT MEASURES (TEAMEASURES)

In 1989, I introduced the first version of Telephone Effectiveness Assessment Measures, also known as (TEAMeasures). This is a comprehensive system for measuring phone call quality and CSR achievement that aspires to fulfilling the ten requirements just enumerated. It has proven to be an excellent technique for assessing, improving, and rewarding customer service transactions. TEAMeasures have been adopted by numerous companies across various industries.

The TEAMeasures system is more than a descriptive tool; it is also prescriptive. Like a recipe for success, it says: "If you do these things, you'll achieve top-notch customer satisfaction, on a consistent basis." Moreover, TEAMeasures can be used to evaluate CSR job applicants. For example, when potential reps inquire about a position, they can be unobtrusively screened in such vital areas as articulation, grammar, vocabulary, general demeanor/cheerfulness, and vocal variety.

THE TEAMEASURES SCORING SYSTEM

The TEAMeasures scoring system includes four general categories: (1) Call Path, (2) Speech/Communication Characteristics, (3) Explanations, and (4) Customer Response. The individual variables that we discussed in Chapter 2 are scored according to the four classifications. Using TEAMeasures, a rep can earn up to 100 points during each conversation.

THE TEAMEASURES DOCUMENTS

Two documents are necessary for implementing the TEAMeasures scoring system. The first document, the TEAMeasures Scoring Sheet, is reproduced on the next pages. This is what reps and managers use to evaluate specific aspects of calls. A second document is used as a guideline for interpreting the call, so the proper scores are assigned. This is called the TEAMeasures Definitions. First, let's take a look at the TEAMeasures Scoring Sheet.

Telephone Effectiveness Assessment Measures (TEAMeasures) Call Scoring Sheet						
Copyright, 1997, Dr. Gary S. Goodman						
Call Path						Comments
Greeting	4	3	2	1	0	
Promise of Help	4	3	2	1	0	
Offer Add'l. Help	4	3	2	1	0	
Rep's Recommitment	4	3	2	1	0	
Speech Characteristics						
General Demeanor/ Cheerfulness	4	3	2	1	0	
Courtesy	4	3	2	1	0	
Articulation	4	3	2	1	0	
Speed	4	3	2	1	0	
Pitch	4	3	2	1	0	
Volume	4	3	2	1	0	
Calibration	4	3	2	1	0	
Vocabulary	4	3	2	1	0	
Grammar	4	3	2	1	0	
Energy	4	3	2	1	0	
Explanations						
Quickness	4	3	2	1	0	
Accuracy	8	6	4	2	0	
Appropriateness/ Relevance	4	3	2	1	0	
Organization	4	3	2	1	0	
Transitions	4	3	2	1	0	

Empathy/ Supportiveness	4	3	2	1	0
Listening/ Active Listening	4	3	2	1	0

Customer Response

Tone	4	3	2	1	0
Gratitude	4	3	2	1	0
Customer's Recommitment	4	3	2	1	0

Scoring:

Possible Points = (100)

Points Earned =

Percentage of Effectiveness =

Strengths & Improvement Objectives:

(1)

(2)

(3)

(4)

(5)

Manager's Summary:

Associate's Summary:

How to Score Calls

There are some special procedures to follow to get the most from the TEAMeasures scoring process. One way to do this is to get reps involved in the procedure as much as they can be.

As you'll recall from Chapter 3, I like to put reps in charge of the tape recording process to create a sense of ownership of the evaluation program. We accomplish this by having reps judge their own calls and record their findings on the TEAMeasures scoring sheet. Afterward, they bring the tape of their calls to their supervisor, manager, or team leader, so the person in charge can also score the same calls. Then, after the manager has finished filling in the scoring sheet, he and the rep get together in a private office or a conference room to replay the conversations and to "compare notes" with regard to their respective scores.

Generally, there is a multipart sequence to this coaching and counseling session. First, Call Path elements are scored, along with the proper Tone and Timing instructions with which they are delivered. The tape will be started at the beginning of call #1. The first question scorers are interested in answering is whether the rep is "on or off the Call Path." So, they'll listen to the Greeting. If it is done on a word-for-word basis, the rep will earn all four of the available points.

On the manager's and the rep's scoring sheets the number "4" should be circled next to the word "Greeting" under the Call Path heading. If there is a different score on either set of pages, someone has erred with respect to tallying his or her score. At that point, a short discussion takes place to see why the perceptions differ.

In measuring Call Path compliance, scorers are asked to simply count the number of words that have been altered by the rep. If she used the right words in the right order, she earns a 4. If she changed one word, the score drops to 3. A two-word alteration makes the score 2. Change three words and the score becomes 1. Drop, add, or substitute four or more words, and a zero is earned on that Call Path attribute.

If you look at the Call Path scoring section, you'll note that there are four basic Call Path attributes. Each attribute can score up to four points, for a total of 16 points available, overall, for Call Path compliance.

It's Easy for Reps to Earn Points

How can a rep earn all 16 points? All she needs to do is make sure she adheres to the language of the Call Path. How can she lose points? Deviate from it. As you can see, from a scoring standpoint, the Call Path category is exceedingly easy to evaluate. If you have a clear tape recording of the call, you won't have any problem scoring this section.

Scoring the Two "T's": Tone and Timing

So far we have discussed the scoring of the content of the call. We've been concerned with whether the rep has used the Call Path language. However, we must also assure that reps say these words with the proper intonation and at the appropriate time.

We'll score tone and timing under the Speech Characteristics category, which is the next major heading in the scoring sheet. Do you recall how the end of the Greeting is supposed to sound? When reps say, "How may I help you?" "you" is supposed to move upward in pitch so much that it is the highest sounding word in the phrase.

What happens if the rep doesn't do this? She'll lose one point under the category "Pitch." If she repeats this problem throughout the Call Path, she may lose all four of her Pitch points. For instance, if her pitch declines instead of ascending during the Promise of Help, Offer of Additional Help, and Recommitment, then each flaw is a scorable event, requiring reps and managers to deduct points from their scoring sheet. Of course, if the rep has used the proper intonation, she'll receive all her Pitch points. It's easy to score the Call Path-related Pitch points right after we have scored the Textual components of the Call Path.

What happens if the rep has used the right words and the proper pitch, but he is late in bringing in parts of the Call Path? We'll score these lapses under the category of "Calibration." You'll recall that timing is important to the Call Path, because it pulls the call together and manages its length. If reps fail to employ the appropriate Timing, it's less likely they'll generate the desired Customer Responses.

So, let's say the rep is late in bringing in the Promise of Help. Instead of saying, "Sure, I'll be happy to help you with that" in a timely way, he waits. In that case, we'll deduct one point from Calibration.

What If the Rep Leaves Out the Entire Promise of Help?

If the rep completely leaves out the Promise of Help, how do we score that aspect of the call? In one sense, he's running very late in inserting it, so we could consider deducting a point from Calibration. But that's not the best place to score this error.

When a rep leaves out the Promise of Help, he loses four points from the Call Path tally. But we don't also "ding" him on Calibration. If we did, this would be considered *double-dipping,* or deducting points from more than one place on the scoring sheet for the same scorable event. Fairness requires that a person be scored only once for each scorable event.

To lose points from more than one category requires that multiple scorable events be involved. If only one event has occurred, then a deduction can be made under only one category.

The Reason There Are Stop-Losses

Reps can lose only that number of points assigned to the respective categories of the scoring sheet. Calibration, as a category, has four points. Therefore, its overall value is only 4% of the scoring system. This value can't increase arbitrarily. For example, if a rep made ten calibration errors, she would still lose only four points, because that is the total number of points provided for under the Calibration category.

The manager will certainly wish to discuss all ten of the lapses with the rep, because this is an obvious problem area that begs for improvement. But we have a "stop-loss" provision that is built into the system. *A rep simply can't be "flunked" on a call because she performs poorly in a single area.*

Example: "Pet Peeves." In most informal coaching and counseling situations, managers may be tempted to become excessive in their criticism. For example, if the manager has a pet peeve that the rep inadvertently triggers, then the rep could be punished unfairly.

I've seen many managers launch into near-tirades about the misuse of a particular word, making it seem that the entire quality of the call hinged on this single error. One manager I worked with flipped out whenever reps inserted too many "okays" at the ends of their lines. She wanted to flunk every rep who committed this linguistic sin. Such abusive criticism can easily go unchecked, unless we have explicit measures that include stop-loss provisions.

Evaluating the Rep's Knowledge and Information Handling

The lion's share of a customer service person's work is spent in communicating, so it's natural that we'd want to pay careful attention to abilities in this area. But, in addition to such process values, a rep's work also entails content.

Reps need to be able to answer questions quickly and thoroughly, and their responses must be truthful and accurate. In other words, our measurement tools need to provide feedback to reps and managers regarding the level of mastery that CSRs have obtained about product and procedural knowledge. TEAMeasures cover this area of evaluation in the Explanations section.

Specifically, we're interested in asking these questions about a rep's performance in a given call: (1) Did the rep offer information to the customer in a suitably prompt manner? If he stumbled or hesitated in such a way as to diminish credibility, making the customer uncomfortable, then a point is deducted. (2) Were the CSRs' points of information accurate? This is an exceedingly important question. If Ms. Smith booked a long airline flight and was informed that she'd be upgraded to business class or first class, instead of riding in economy class, she would be very disappointed if she arrived at the airport and was told that she had been misinformed by the reservations agent.

Because so much good will and company revenue depend on the accuracy of the information given by reps, many of my clients have double-weighted this TEAMeasures category. So, instead of deducting a single point for inaccuracies, they deduct two points at a time. The stop-loss on points is set at eight, instead of the customary four points.

Another important content dimension of TEAMeasures is referred to as *appropriateness/relevance*. This measure raises a few questions. Did the CSR offer a thorough explanation? Did the customer receive a clear message as to what to expect? And did the rep stay on the topic, or did she wander and answer a question that wasn't really asked?

Example Revisited: Previously I mentioned the story of the rep who gave an incomplete answer to a customer. I'd like to augment that example to show you how a number of scorable events are handled within the same transaction.

A mutual fund customer called to discover the reason he hadn't received his customary, semiannual account statement. After being greeted by the CSR, the conversation went as follows:

"It seems I used to get a dividend at least twice a year. Has that changed?"

"Yes, sir."

"You see, I was getting a little concerned . . ."

"Yes, the dividend will be paid once, annually, on the 15th."

"Of December?"

"Yes, sir."

"Oh, okay, because I was getting concerned . . ."

When the customer asked, "has the dividend changed?" the rep could have offered more of an explanation than, "Yes, sir." Likewise, the CSR shouldn't have omitted the month when the dividend would be paid. The entire answer should have been:

Sure, I'll be happy to help you with that. The dividend has been changed. It will be paid once, annually, on the 15th of December, and is there anything else I can help you with?

I "wrapped" the Call Path around the CSR's answer, didn't I? That's exactly how a rep should do it, to produce the most positive effect. By replying, immediately, with "Sure, I'll be happy to help you with that . . ." the rep would put this client at ease. After all, if the client thinks his investment company has been "skipping dividends," he might be a little uptight, right? So, using the Promise of Help would buoy his confidence in the rep as well as in her company.

Then, she should have followed with a complete and clear answer. Once the client had been informed about the new dividend date, she should have bundled-up the call with the Offer of Additional Help.

How Many Points Did This Rep Lose?

If it seems to you that the rep in this example must have lost a fair number of TEAMeasures points, you're right. How many points do you think we should deduct?

Let's walk through the scoring together, by referring back to the text in the example:

It seems I used to get a dividend at least twice a year. Has that changed?
Yes, sir.

This is the first time at which points are deducted, that is, it is the first scorable event. Do you know the reason? Hint: What is the CSR supposed to say after a customer has made an opening statement or has asked a question? That's right. "Sure, I'll be happy to help you with that . . . " However, the rep simply answered with a "Yes, sir." She should have said: "Sure, I'll be happy to help you with that. The dividend payment date has been changed."

So, how many points does she lose, and under which categories is she scored for this lapse? Well, she left out the entire Promise of Help, so she'll lose four points from the Promise of Help category on TEAMeasures.

Let's move to the next scorable event, which is triggered by this dialogue:

You see, I was getting a little concerned . . .
Yes, the dividend will be paid once, annually, on the 15th.

There are two scorable events that come into play at this point. First, the CSR gave an incomplete answer with the words "on the 15th"; she should have said, "on the 15th of December." This lapse is scored under the heading Appropriateness/Relevance. One point is deducted there.

The second scorable event occurred when the rep failed to tie her answer together with an Offer of Additional Help. If she's simply running late in inserting it, she loses one point for Calibration. If she leaves this Call Path element out entirely, she'll lose four points under the Call Path heading.

Scoring Is Made Accurate with the Proper Definitions

To this point, I have introduced a few of the variables that are included in the TEAMeasures scoring system. They've given you an initial understanding of how the program works. This would be a good time to introduce to you the entire set of TEAMeasures Definitions. They will enable you to define scorable events in conversations and provide CSRs with a full evaluation of their conversations with customers. I suggest you invest at least a half-hour reading through them, the first time around.

Telephone Effectiveness Assessment Measures (TEAMeasures)
Definitions
Copyright 1997, Dr. Gary S. Goodman

Call Path

Comments:

The first four measures are concerned with the extent to which the Call Path is used. If it is used on a word-for-word basis throughout the Greeting, Promise of Help, Offer of Additional Help, and Recommitment, four points are awarded for each segment, or 16 points total.

If one word is changed, eliminated, or added, the score drops to 3. If two words are affected, the score drops to 2; changing three words drops the score to 1. Changing four words or more, or complete omission, earns no points.

Note: The Call Path, to evoke optimal customer response, needs to be performed with the stair-stepped tones taught in training. Tone is not—repeat, not—assessed in the first four measures dealing with the Call Path. Tone is evaluated through the measures associated with the category Speech Characteristics.

Greeting	4	3	2	1	0
Promise of Help	4	3	2	1	0
Offer Add'l. Help	4	3	2	1	0
Recommitment	4	3	2	1	0

Speech Characteristics

General Demeanor/ Cheerfulness	4	3	2	1	0

Comments:

Does the voice have an optimistic, upbeat, up-tempo quality? Do the ends of lines, as well as tones during transitions, sound bright and pleasant, or do they descend, giving the impression of a speaker who is dispirited, irritated, or out of sorts? Does this person sound happy doing what he is doing?

Courtesy   4   3   2   1   0

Comments:

Courtesy is typified by the frequent use of terms such as "please" and "thank you." Does the speaker show consideration and thoughtfulness for the feelings and comfort of the client? Placing people on hold requires courtesy. "May I ask you to hold for a moment, please?" is strong on courtesy, while "Can you hold?" or "One moment" lack courtesy. Courtesy is most often demonstrated during the "middle" of the conversation when reps are selecting their own words in speaking with customers. Overt rudeness would be scored at 0, and the absence of appropriate courtesy would be rated between 1–3. Appropriate courtesy is rated at 4.

Articulation   4   3   2   1   0

Comments:

Articulation is the clear vocalization and pronunciation of words. Good articulation at a 4 level occurs when the rep's language is fully formed and completely understood by a listener of reasonable sensibilities. A sign of problematic articulation is when the client repeatedly asks the rep to repeat herself or when confusion seems to result from words poorly transmitted and therefore poorly received. Note: Some listeners have physiological problems that affect hearing, and some phone calls are poorly amplified. These factors should be ruled out as scorable events if the problem persists across several calls.

Speed   4   3   2   1   0

Comments:

Does the speaker speak at an unusually fast or slow rate? (Note: Average speed is 100–150 words per minute.) To what extent is this factor diminishing the rep's effectiveness?

Pitch   4   3   2   1   0

Comments:

Has the rep's intonation sufficient variety? Is it appropriate? In the "middle" of the call, does the rep use enough variety in her tone of voice to sustain a reasonable person's attention and interest? Or does she use a monotone or an excessively sing-song pattern? When doing the Call Path, does the rep use the stair-step upward-pitch technique she learned in training?

Volume   4   3   2   1   0

Comments:

Does the speaker speak in an unusually loud or soft manner? [Standard: Can the speaker be heard 5–7 feet away (when assessing softness) or as far away as 15–20 feet (when assessing loudness)?]

Calibration   4   3   2   1   0

Comments:

Does the rep match his comments to those of the customer in such a manner as to give an appropriate give-and-take, turn-taking aspect to the call? Or, does the rep speak when the client is speaking, or stay silent when the other party is silent, thus creating annoying overlaps or pauses in the conversation? A well-calibrated conversation is freely flowing, comfortable, and apparently effortless on the part of both participants. It is a true dialogue—not two simultaneous monologues. A late insertion of a part of the Call Path is a calibration problem, as well.

Vocabulary   4   3   2   1   0

Comments:

Does the rep use appropriate words to describe procedures and provide explanations to clients? Or, does he hesitate frequently in a search for words?

Grammar   4   3   2   1   0

Comments:

Does the speaker make grammatical errors? Typical errors include subject/verb disagreement, for example, "He don't," or singular/plural mistakes such as "Three item on back-order" and using "criterion" instead of "criteria."

Energy	4	3	2	1	0

Comments:

Does the rep infuse his speech with consistent vitality, or does he sound listless or lethargic? (Energy may co-vary with volume. A soft voice may be associated with low energy, whereas a loud voice may be associated with high energy.)

Explanations

Quickness	4	3	2	1	0

How fast does the rep provide information?

Accuracy	8	6	4	2	0

How valid or truthful is the information delivered by the rep? Is the rep unduly vague or ambiguous in her explanations?

Appropriateness/ Relevance	4	3	2	1	0

Is the information given or requested by the rep appropriate to the requirement of a particular call? Does the rep ask appropriate questions to get the information he needs to assist the customer? Does the rep overexplain or underexplain?

Organization	4	3	2	1	0

Does the rep order her ideas in a coherent, easily understood manner? When desirable, does she use the PEP format for organizing answers to common questions? Example: "Why is a signature guarantee necessary?" or "How do I get a signature guarantee?"

Transitions	4	3	2	1	0

Transitions are the connecting words and phrases that provide a bridge from one part of the conversation to the next. Sometimes referred to as "fillers," they reduce the number of lulls in the exchange. Example: "May I ask you to hold for a moment while I bring that up on my screen?" or "This may take just a quick second to enter for you—May I ask you to hold?" Formal transition phrases also apply here: "Well, I understand that, but . . ." and "Well I appreciate that, but . . ." (See page 3 of Call Path documents for more examples of transition phrases.)

Empathy/   4   3   2   1   0
  Supportiveness

Empathy is a showing of concern on the part of a rep for the circumstances of the client. "I'm sorry to hear that," is an empathic statement; "I know what you mean," is another example. There are two ways to be supportive: (1) by using supportive messages and (2) by avoiding defensive messages. The following factors are involved in supportive messages: (a) description; (b) problem and solution orientation; (c) spontaneity; (d) equality; and (e) flexibility. Defensive messages involve (a) evaluation; (b) control; (c) strategy; (d) neutrality; (e) superiority; and (f) certainty.

Listening/   4   3   2   1   0
  Active Listening

When we listen effectively, we process information the first time we hear it. If a customer says at the beginning of a call that he wants to check on an order, and, on bringing the account up on the screen the rep has to ask, "And how may I help you?" then she has not been listening effectively. To determine whether we listened correctly, we should use active listening, whereby we repeat the meaning we believe the caller conveyed to us.

Customer Response

Our goal is to make customers happy and to have them express words of gratitude to us and recommit to doing business with our company. These three measures allow us to assess what the customers say to us and the tone they use as the conversation comes to a close.

Tone   4   3   2   1   0

Does the customer "sing" back to us? Is there a noticeable presence of lightness, or upward movement to the customer's tone of voice, as he responds to the question "And is there anything else I can help you with this morning/afternoon?" In his response, if the upward movement of his tone of voice reaches a high point in his vocal range, the rep earns four points. A significant, positive upward movement, though less extreme, earns three points. A moderate upward movement earns two points. A very slight upward movement earns one point. If the customer's tone fails to move up, no points are earned. A downward or negative movement also earns no points.

Gratitude   4   3   2   1   0

How does the customer express her appreciation of the rep's efforts? "Thank you," "Thanks," or "Have a nice day," are sufficient to earn one point. "I appreciate it" earns two points. "You've been a lot of help," earns three points. "You're terrific," "You've done more than enough," "You're wonderful," and equivalent expressions earn four points.

Recommitment   4   3   2   1   0

Words of recommitment are usually uttered after we thank the client for doing business with our company. If the customer vows to do additional business with us, this is definitely recommitment at a 4 level. If the person says "You bet!" or "Sure thing," or "Absolutely," the rep scores three points. A response of "okay" or "all right" merits a score of 2, while "un-huh" merits a score of 1.

Scoring: Possible Points   =   (100)

                     Points Earned   =

                     Percentage of Effectiveness   =

Improvement Objectives:

(1)

(2)

(3)

(4)

(5)

Summary:

Associate's Response:

Additional Comments Regarding TEAMeasures

As you know, every effort is made in the TEAMeasures system to successfully operationalize definitions. This bears fruit when assessing General Demeanor/Cheerfulness. Instead of focusing on the question, "Is this a nice and cheerful rep?" our interest is rooted in behavior. We inquire into what the rep is doing with her voice. If her "lines" end in an ascending tone and they "crest," she is, by definition, sounding cheerful. If, however, her tone descends, she is projecting an image of a CSR who is dispirited or out of sorts.

An emphasis on vocal behavior enables the manager and the rep to avoid the sticky wicket of trying to define a CSR's "essence." For example, when coaching a rep, it would be a mistake for the manager to assert, "You're such a cheerful person!" This statement would pin a label on the rep and make it appear that, because she is cheerful, she always acts that way, and she wouldn't or couldn't act in another way. This isn't a realistic portrait of a complex human being, and it isn't a helpful way to provide feedback.

What the manager should be doing is defining, in action terms, exactly what the rep is doing to come across to customers as being "cheerful." Once that behavior is defined, the rep can consciously do more of it. If she arrives at work feeling bad, she can still choose to behave toward customers as if she's perfectly all right.

In a similar vein, what if the manager suspects that there is something disturbing about the rep's manner. It would be unfair to flatly say, "Terri just seems to rub some people the wrong way" and leave the commentary at that superficial level. A manager who is using TEAMeasures can discover exactly what is causing Terri to come across that way by using the Empathy/Supportiveness category. Possibly, Terri is sounding sarcastic, and, until this point, no one had diagnosed her problem. Terri could be completely unaware of this tendency. But she can be coached to alter her intonation pattern, so it sounds more sincere.

We Should Respect Certain "Boundaries" When Using TEAMeasures

It is entirely possible that Terri is a very sincere individual, but she seldom comes across that way. It's ironic, isn't it? She could feel exceedingly customer-oriented and believe she is being nothing-but-helpful, yet she could still miscommunicate these positive intentions. So, Terri needs to be taught how to sound sincere, despite the fact that she may already be sincere. By the same logic, someone could be insincere, yet appear to customers as one of the most genuine individuals on earth. It doesn't seem fair, does it?

But these are real-world contradictions that managers must contend with. And, in the final analysis, it shouldn't be the manager's role to determine who is or isn't really sincere or cheerful. As long as a rep can perform the behaviors that make the best impressions on customers, the rep's internal, psychological state is off-bounds to the manager. It should be considered as private an area as one's spiritual or political beliefs.

Scoring the TEAMeasures Sheets

Assuming that an entire phone call is being measured, all 100 TEAMeasures points will be involved in the scoring session; 16 points will be scored for the Call Path; 40 points for Speech Characteristics; 32 points for Explanations; and 12 points for Customer Response. Here are the scoring "assumptions" that the manager should use as she approaches each one of these sections.

1. *Call Path points:* A rep must earn these points by proactively using the exact words of the Call Path. By dropping, changing, or altering words, reps lose points.

2. *Speech Characteristics points:* Reps lose points by committing communication errors. However, a CSR will be awarded all four Vocabulary points as a matter of course, if his word choices are appropriate. An exception occurs with regard to some of the points under the Pitch heading. A CSR must perform the Call Path with a rising voice pitch pattern. If she doesn't do this, she'll lose a point for each error.

3. *Explanations points:* The rep is presumed to be earning these points. We will also assume her Listening was effective, if there are no scorable events to the contrary.

4. *Customer Response points:* As with the Call Path points, a rep must proactively earn the points available under Customer Response. A rep causes a client to thank her, to sing, and to recommit. If these things don't occur, or they occur with less intensity than we wish, the rep loses points.

General TEAMeasures Scoring Principles

There are some general scoring principles that apply to using TEAMeasures in performance evaluations:

(1) *In a scoring situation in which there is a difference of one point separating the rep's score from the manager's score, the rep will usually be given the benefit of the doubt and be awarded the extra point.*

Example: Possibly the most difficult category to score is the one that deals with measuring the amount of "singing" that a customer does as he responds to the Call Path question "And is there anything else I can help you with?"

A quick look at the Customer Response segment's definition of Tone illustrates the challenge:

Tone   4   3   2   1   0

Does the customer "sing" back to us? Is there a noticeable presence of lightness or upward movement to his voice pitch as he responds to the question "And is there anything else I can help you with this morning/afternoon?" If the customer's ascending tone is at a high point in his vocal range, the rep earns four points. A significant, positive upward movement, though less extreme, earns three points. A moderate upward movement earns two points. A very slight upward movement earns one point. If the tone fails to move up, no points are earned. A downward or negative movement also earns no points.

After replaying the tape of a customer's response, reps and managers usually score Tone similarly. The manager might say that the customer's "singing" was at a 2–level, while the rep believes it was at a 3–level.

Seldom will the "spread" between scores be more than one point, or possibly two points. I've never seen a manager score Tone at 0 or 1 while the rep has scored it at 4.

As part of the coaching and counseling session, CSRs and managers are asked to arrive at a consensus with regard to the scoring of all TEAMeasures; it is then an easy matter to set future performance objectives. If there is a disagreement between the manager and the CSR over a score, it is usually best to award the higher score to the CSR. Why do we do this? It is to motivate the rep and to demonstrate that the overall intent of the evaluation system is to reward, rather than to punish, behavior.

(2) *If two TEAMeasures categories could apply to one scorable event, the one that should be used is the one that is more prescriptive for the rep's future behavior.*

Example: A customer calls to find out when her shipment is scheduled to arrive. Claire's computer is running slowly, so there is a very long and uncomfortable pause while she waits for the appropriate data to appear on her screen. The customer begins to worry. "Have they lost it? Has it even been shipped, yet?

Which two TEAMeasures categories could apply to this scorable event: the uncomfortable pause?

If you said Calibration and Transitions, you'd be right. Let's review these to see how they might apply to scoring this situation.

Calibration	4	3	2	1	0

Comments:

Does the rep match his comments to those of the customer in such a manner as to give an appropriate give-and-take, turn-taking aspect to the call? Or does he speak when the client is speaking, or is he silent when the customer is silent, thus creating annoying overlaps or pauses in the conversation? A well-calibrated conversation is freely flowing, comfortable, and apparently effortless. It is a true dialogue—not two simultaneous monologues. A late insertion of a part of the Call Path is a calibration problem, as well.

The critical phrase is "thus creating annoying overlaps or pauses in the conversation." Claire's pause was annoying, wasn't it? It made the customer worry, and one of our key goals in using the Call Path is to reduce customer apprehension.

Now, let's turn to Transition.

Transition	4	3	2	1	0

Transitions are the connecting words and phrases that provide a bridge from one part of the conversation to the next. Sometimes referred to as "fillers," they reduce the number of lulls in the exchange. Examples are "May I ask you to hold for a moment while I bring that up on my screen?" and "This may take just a quick second to enter for you—May I ask you to hold?" Formal transition phrases also apply here: "Well, I understand that but . . ." and "Well, I appreciate that, but . . ." (See page 3 of Call Path documents for more examples of transition phrases.)

Aha! This category, more than Calibration, applies to the example of Claire. It instructs reps to insert "fillers" to "reduce the number of lulls in the exchange." Claire could have volunteered that "This may take just an extra second or two to bring up on my screen because my computer is a little slow this morning."

For the scorable event depicted in this example, Transitions is the better category to use because it tells reps what to do to avoid making the error in the future. In other words, it is more than simply descriptive of the problem—it actually supplies a prescription—a solution.

So, once again, if two categories seem to apply, examine them closely before deciding which one to use. Then, try to select the one that is more helpful to the rep, after discussing both of them openly and completely. And, of course, we should never double-dip by scoring the rep down in two categories if they both refer to one scorable event.

Scorable Events Can Quickly Stack Up

Managers should be alert to each and every scorable event, even if it seems like they are breaking a lot of "bad news" to the rep all at once. Remember, the best hope we have for significantly improving customer service is by being thorough and persistent in pointing out both strengths and weaknesses. Then, reps can be on clear notice about what they need to maintain and what they need to work on.

Example: The Greeting can contain a number of errors that seem to occur at the same time. Here's how it should be done:

Hello, Goodman Communications, this is Gary on a recorded line. How may I help you?

But what if the rep, in all innocence, says:

Good morning, Goodman Communications, this is Gary on a recorded line. How may I help you?

How many points can the rep lose?

Based on saying "Good morning" instead of "Hello," she'd lose two Call Path points for altering two words. But that's just where the scoring begins. Remember that we also need to score Tone and Timing.

There are three distinct instructions for the rep to follow in performing the Pitch. Her voice should rise and hit a first peak with the words "Goodman Communications." Next, her tone should go down the stairs as she says "on a recorded line." Finally, her tone should go up to a final crescendo as she says, "How may I help *you*?"

We teach reps to use this three-part pitch technique to make the disclosure about recording sound less threatening. By making her tone descend at the critical point, the rep subliminally tells the customer, "This information isn't really important, so you can ignore it."

If the CSR gets all three pitch movements right, she'll retain all of her Pitch points. But if she isn't concentrating, it will be easy for her to reverse the order. Instead of moving

    up———down———up,

she'll err by moving

    down———up———down.

If that happens, we'll deduct three points for Pitch, because each tonal error in the Greeting constitutes a scorable event.

Do You Think That's Too Harsh?

At this point, I wouldn't blame you if you were thinking, "That seems harsh." But let's put these errors into perspective. You'll want to do this over and over again, for the benefit of your reps, your fellow managers, and yourself.

There is a crucial, reality-testing question that I encourage you to ask whenever you consider whether a communications phenomenon should be a scorable event: *Could this event have had an adverse effect on the customer?* In other words, is the rep's apparent error "a difference that makes a difference?" Let's apply this test to the three-point deduction that we'd make from the score of the rep who didn't follow the three Pitch instructions in the Greeting.

(1) The first instruction is for the rep to move her voice upward when she says, "Goodman Communications." Is there a good reason for doing this? Absolutely. By raising her voice pitch, she's conveying an upbeat, enthusiastic impression. The importance of the "cresting" of the rep's voice is delineated by the General Demeanor/Cheerfulness TEAMeasures category.

Another way to dramatize the importance of this tonal instruction is to ask "What would happen if she did it the opposite way—if her tone descended at that point?" Would it sound bleak and dispirited?

(2) The second tonal instruction is to make one's voice move downward when delivering the phrase "on a recorded line." This is crucial for reps to do, because if they raise their voice pitch, they'll needlessly induce customers to inquire about

the recording process and its necessity. In other words, if the rep's tone descends as it should, it will make the idea of recording sound like it is a standard operating procedure. Otherwise customers will ask, "Why are you recording this call?" They'll question the practice because the rep's tone will sound as if he is questioning the company's practice. In other words, clients will adopt the rep's attitude, one way or the other, so he needs to be sure he's projecting the proper one.

(3) In a previous section, I mentioned the importance of hitting a tonal crescendo when the rep says, "How may I help you?" By raising voice pitch, the rep sends a signal that she sincerely wants to help, and that she's looking forward to what will follow in the conversation. Again, if the rep sends an optimistic signal, the customer is likely to adopt an optimistic attitude.

As you can see from these three explanations, there are good reasons for scoring reps for each event in the Call Path. It is essential that managers be ready, willing, and able to repeatedly do what I just did here. They need to *justify* the necessity of using the Call Path, Text, Tone, and Timing instructions, as well as the TEAMeasures process.

Additional Points Can Be Involved

The rep could lose even more points for a botched Greeting. Here are four possibilities:

1. Her speech could be too fast or too slow;

2. Her articulation could suffer if

   • she doesn't accurately pronounce the words of the Call Path;

   •her energy plummets;

   • her volume becomes too loud or too soft.

Of course, most of these points apply to the entire conversation; they don't apply exclusively to the Greeting.

Under actual scoring conditions, most reps score most of the points. In fact, you'll find that average CSRs will earn at least a C+, or 75–level, on TEAMeasures, providing they invest at least a moderate effort in doing what we train them to do. My clients usually score in the 82–84% range immediately after reps and managers have completed their training. Then, our goal becomes attaining a staff average of 90% or above.

Which Is the Scorable Unit: The Word or the Phrase?

When we score a conversation, do we focus on entire sentences or on individual words? The answer varies depending on the category being assessed. For example, if we're scoring Articulation, we'll focus on whether individual words, or even syllables, have been properly pronounced. But when we score Pitch and Speed, we have to examine entire phrases to make our judgments in the proper contexts.

"Red-Flag" TEAMeasures Categories

No system for measuring telephone effectiveness or customer service is perfect, including TEAMeasures. One of the drawbacks of TEAMeasures is the fact that a CSR could commit an error that is so problematic for a given customer, or for certain types of customers, that the error wouldn't be appropriately evaluated. For example, if a CSR were overtly rude to a customer, he would probably be penalized on a number of dimensions, including General Demeanor/Cheerfulness, Politeness, and Empathy/Supportiveness. However, his or her final score might not completely reflect the damage he did to the company's relationship with the customer.

Using TEAMeasures as a Recruiting Tool

You may also wish to use TEAMeasures as a CSR recruiting and screening tool. CSR job applicants can be required to go through at least one telephone interview before being granted a "live" one. During the interview, or afterward if it has been taped, the manager can evaluate the prospective rep's potential by scoring certain TEAMeasures categories. For example, nearly all of the Speech Characteristics categories could be pertinent. Here is a review.

Speech Characteristics

General Demeanor/ Cheerfulness	4	3	2	1	0

Comments:

Does the voice have an optimistic, upbeat, up-tempo quality? Do the ends of lines, as well as tones during transitions, sound bright and pleasant, or do they descend, giving the impression of a speaker who is dispirited, irritated, or out of sorts? Does this person sound happy doing what he is doing?

Courtesy		4	3	2	1	0

Comments:

Courtesy is typified by the frequent use of terms such as "please" and "thank you." Does the speaker show consideration and thoughtfulness for the feelings and comfort of the client? Placing people on hold requires courtesy. "May I ask you to hold for a moment, please?" is strong on courtesy, while "Can you hold?" or "One moment" lack courtesy. Courtesy is most often demonstrated during the "middle" of the conversation when reps are selecting their own words in speaking with customers. Overt rudeness would be scored at 0, and the absence of appropriate courtesy would be rated between 1–3. Appropriate courtesy is rated at 4.

Articulation		4	3	2	1	0

Comments:

Articulation is the clear vocalization and pronunciation of words. Good articulation at a 4 level occurs when the rep's language is fully formed and completely understood by a listener of reasonable sensibilities. A sign of problematic articulation is when the client repeatedly asks the rep to repeat herself, or when confusion seems to result from words poorly transmitted and therefore poorly received. Note: Some listeners have physiological problems that affect hearing, and some phone calls are poorly amplified. These factors should be ruled out as scorable events.

Speed		4	3	2	1	0

Comments:

Does the speaker speak at an unusually fast or slow rate? (Note: Average speed is reported at 100–150 words per minute.) To what extent is this factor diminishing the rep's effectiveness?

Pitch		4	3	2	1	0

Comments:

Have the rep's intonations sufficient variety? Are they appropriate? In the "middle" of the call, does the rep use enough variety in her tone of voice to sustain a reasonable person's attention and interest? Or does she use a monotone or an excessively sing-song pattern? When doing the Call Path, does the rep use the stair-step upward pitch technique she learned in training?

Volume   4   3   2   1   0

Comments:

Does the speaker speak in an unusually loud or soft manner? [(Standard: Can the speaker be heard 5–7 feet away (when assessing softness) or as far away as 15–20 feet (when assessing loudness)?]

Calibration   4   3   2   1   0

Comments:

Does the rep match his comments to those of the customer in such a manner as to give an appropriate give-and-take, turn-taking aspect to the call? Or does the rep speak when the client is speaking, or stay silent when the customer is silent, thus creating annoying overlaps or pauses in the conversation? A well-calibrated conversation is freely flowing, comfortable, and apparently effortless on the part of both parties. It is a true dialogue—not two, simultaneous monologues. A late insertion of a part of the Call Path is a calibration problem, as well.

Vocabulary   4   3   2   1   0

Comments:

Does the rep use appropriate words to describe procedures and provide explanations to clients? Or does he hesitate frequently in a search for words?

Grammar   4   3   2   1   0

Comments:

Does the speaker make grammatical errors? Typical errors include subject/verb disagreements, for example. "He don't," or singular/plural mistakes such as "Three item on back-order" and using "criterion" instead of "criteria."

Energy   4   3   2   1   0

Comments:

Does the rep infuse his speech with consistent vitality, or does he sound listless or lethargic? (Energy may co-vary with volume. A soft voice may be associated with low energy, whereas a loud voice may be associated with high energy.)

Transforming TEAMeasures into Percentage Values

These preceding ten categories can easily be transformed into a 100-point evaluation system by assigning ten points to each one. For example, Pitch would appear as follows on the scoring sheet.

Pitch	10	7.5	5	2.5	0

I favor using 100-point "percentage" scoring systems because so many of us have used them, in one form or another, in measuring achievement. Most of us think of 90–100% as an "A," 80–89% as a "B", and so forth, so these systems are intuitively familiar and comfortable.

When assessing a potential hire's capabilities, you might want to include some of the categories in the Explanations section of TEAMeasures. Let's review them to determine how they can help. Replace the word "rep" with "candidate," and you can see how helpful these categories can be in an employee-screening context.

Explanations

Quickness	4	3	2	1	0

How fast does the candidate provide information?

Accuracy	8	6	4	2	0

How valid or truthful is the information delivered by the candidate? Is she unduly vague or ambiguous in her explanations?

Appropriateness/ Relevance	4	3	2	1	0

Is the information given or requested by the candidate appropriate to the particular call? Does he ask appropriate questions to get the information he needs to assist the customer? Does he overexplain or underexplain?

Organization	4	3	2	1	0

Does the candidate order her ideas in a coherent, easily understood manner? When desirable, does she use the PEP format for organizing answers to common questions?

Transitions	4	3	2	1	0

These are the connecting words and phrases that provide a bridge from one part of the conversation to the next. Sometimes referred to as "fillers," they reduce the number of lulls in the exchange. Example: "May I ask you to hold for a moment while I bring that up on my screen?" or "This may take just a quick second to enter for you—May I ask you to hold?" Formal transition phrases also apply here: "Well, I understand that but . . ." and "Well, I appreciate that, but . . ." See page 3 of Call Path documents for more examples of transition phrases.

| Empathy/ | 4 | 3 | 2 | 1 | 0 |
| Supportiveness | | | | | |

Empathy is a showing of concern on the part of the candidate for the circumstances of the client. "I'm sorry to hear that" is an empathic statement. "I know what you mean" is another. There are two ways to be supportive: (1) by using supportive messages and (2) by avoiding defensive messages. Supportive messages involve the following factors: (a) description; (b) problem and solution orientation; (c) spontaneity; (d) equality; and (e) flexibility. Defensive messages involve (a) evaluation; (b) control; (c) strategy; (d) neutrality; (e) superiority; and (f) certainty.

| Listening/ | 4 | 3 | 2 | 1 | 0 |
| Active Listening | | | | | |

When we listen effectively, we process information the first time we hear it. If a customer says at the beginning of a call that he wants to check on an order, and on bringing the account up on the screen the candidate has to ask, "And how may I help you?" then listening has been less than effective. We should always use active listening, during which we repeat the meaning we believe the caller tried to convey.

Are there any Explanations variables that wouldn't be a good fit in employee screening? I don't see any that would be irrelevant, and most of them could be very helpful in evaluating the merit of a potential employee. For example, do you want people who are going to respond *quickly* to the requests of clients? How about people who are going to try to be *accurate* and *truthful*? Should reps have a good sense of time management, in order to handle high call volumes? Then we'll be interested in knowing whether they can answer questions in an *appropriate* and *relevant* manner.

Organized people have a better chance of succeeding in customer service than those who seem to bob and weave all over the conversational landscape. A job candidate should also have an intuitive sense as to when conversations have bogged down, so they'll be likely to spontaneously use *transitions* and other fillers.

We definitely want *empathic* communicators who appreciate the importance of coming across in a *supportive*, not a defensive, manner. And, of course, we want to avoid hiring people who are obviously poor *listeners,* who make us repeat ourselves or answer questions that haven't been asked.

So, we can see that all of the Explanations measures are relevant in evaluating the merit of potential employees.

Additional Thoughts About the TEAMeasures System

Measuring the quality and effectiveness of service-sector individuals is a relatively new field. Initiated in the 1980s by the "Total Quality" movement, and bolstered by the downsizing and re-engineering trends of the 1990s, the idea of carefully managing conversational techniques and outcomes is really catching on.

As a system, TEAMeasures makes customer service work more consistently effective by explicitly defining the range of behaviors that constitute the quality of a job.

For the first time, a rep can say, "I'm excellent at what I do," and have statistical validation for this claim. She can qualify to receive merit pay for work well done, and managers can distribute rewards in appropriate and completely defensible ways.

Managers who have improved the performance of their reps can also ask for reward-compensation. They can say: "I've taken my people from an 80% average to a 90% average, in two quarters!"

Because the TEAMeasures system strives to be an objective one, claims such as these can be externally and internally verified. For people who love the idea of knowing how they rate and feeling that they're making a measurable contribution to the well being of the firm, the TEAMeasures system is a true blessing.

You might get the impression that I think most reps are not being evaluated at present. That's not my belief. They are being measured but more "from the gut" than by a dispassionate and fair set of standards. This situation can lead to problems, especially when managers try to discipline or terminate unproductive individuals.

Until we have explicit, reasonable, and universally enforced standards that are related directly to the work and not to personalities, we could be inviting costly legal actions from disgruntled reps, who might conclude that they have been fired without just cause.

Using TEAMeasures on a regular basis, managers can document and correct performance problems quickly. If improvement is not forthcoming, TEAMeasures scoring sheets can be used as evidence of good-faith efforts to help reps to succeed. They can also show a deterioration in performance and the failure to meet explicit, agreed-on objectives for improvement.

So, TEAMeasures can be used as life-cycle documents, inasmuch as they can be used in screening potential reps, in training and evaluating existing reps, and in termination proceedings. I should point out that implementing a system such as TEAMeasures requires a substantial commitment, in terms of dollars and effort. But there is usually an immediate payback in terms of increased productivity. A substantial amount of management attention will also need to be invested in perpetuating the program, much of it allocated to the coaching and counseling process.

Reps will need to be monitored and measured, but team leaders, supervisors, and managers will have to be evaluated as well. In the next chapter we'll examine the specific responsibilities of these staff members, and we'll introduce a measurement system dedicated to providing them with appropriate feedback and rewards. This system is called SEAmeasures, which is short for Supervisor Effectiveness Assessment Measures. What TEAMeasures does for reps, SEAmeasures does for managers. By employing them, we'll close the circle and enable everyone's performance in the customer service unit to be fairly and appropriately monitored, measured, and managed.

CHAPTER

FIVE

Measuring and Managing Team Leaders, Supervisors, and Customer Service Managers

In previous chapters we discussed some of the critical practices involved in monitoring and measuring front-line customer service activity. In this chapter, we're going to look closely at how we should measure and manage the managers of the service unit. Along the way, we'll be addressing these questions:

1. How can managers implement and sustain the Call Path and TEAMeasures systems that we've introduced? And,

2. How can we evaluate the contributions of managers, so they can be recognized and be rewarded appropriately?

It's one thing to tell your reps: "Starting today, we're going to carefully monitor, measure, and manage your performance." It's quite another to add: "And our achievement as managers will also be monitored, measured, and managed right along with yours. If you don't achieve, neither will we. And if we succeed, we'll succeed, together."

Is there any rational reason our professional "fates" shouldn't be closely linked to the performance of our people? How equitable would it be to set up an evaluation system whereby a manager could obtain hefty raises and promotions while the performance of her reps suffered? Likewise, how would a manager feel if her efforts went unrewarded despite the fact that she truly developed her people's abilities and achievement level?

This chapter offers a system for avoiding these unfair outcomes by operationalizing what effective customer service managers do, just as we operationalized what effective CSRs do. I'm going to introduce a tool that works much like TEAMeasures. It's called SEAmeasures, or Supervisor Effectiveness Assessment Measures. SEAmeasures provide the company with a means of making sure that service quality remains high, by involving all levels of service management in self-scrutiny as well as in accountability to others.

SEAMEASURES: AN OVERVIEW

The SEAmeasures system works much like TEAMeasures. It is a scoring system that focuses on three significant aspects of the work of team leaders, supervisors, and managers. It assesses how well they execute: (1) formal coaching and counseling; (2) the TEAMeasures scoring system; and (3) informal coaching and counseling when they're in the service center or departmental environment.

Because there are 16 SEAmeasures variables, the total number of "raw" points that can be earned is 64. Therefore, after all the raw points are added together, they are multiplied by a factor of 1.5625 to convert the raw score into a percentage score. For example, if a manager earns 58 raw points, this will convert into a total percentage score of 90.625, which is the equivalent of a low "A" rating. As with reps, managers will set objectives with their managers or evaluators, so that they can maintain their strengths and improve their weaknesses.

Unlike TEAMeasures, SEAmeasures uses a single document for scoring calls and for interpreting the definitions that are provided. Following is an initial look at the SEAmeasures instrument.

Supervisor Effectiveness Assessment Measures
(SEAmeasures) Definitions
Copyright, 1991, 1995, 1999 Telephone Effectiveness Institute

Formal Coaching and Counseling

organization   4   3   2   1   0

Does the supervisor provide an overview at the beginning of the session? Does his commentary follow an announced pattern (that is, Call Path elements first, then Customer Response, then Speech Characteristics)?

participation   4   3   2   1   0

Does the supervisor balance the session with her perceptions as well as use questions properly to involve the rep?

nonverbal   4   3   2   1   0
  communication

Does the supervisor use body and facial expressions as well as vocal tone to create a positive atmosphere for rep evaluation?

feedback   4   3   2   1   0

Does the supervisor provide appropriate criticism that emphasizes both the positive and the negative and explains its significance? Or does the supervisor merely announce what he likes or dislikes without explaining effects on the customer or company? Does the supervisor balance his criticism as to identify strengths as well as weaknesses in the rep's performance?

establishing   4   3   2   1   0
  standards

To what extent are group/individual goals for performance made known to the rep? Is the rep made aware of existing as well as targeted group averages on the TEAMeasures?

creating   4   3   2   1   0
  clarity

Does the supervisor use simple, clear, and unambiguous language to explain points and to elucidate principles?

| promoting responsibility | 4 | 3 | 2 | 1 | 0 |

Does the supervisor instill a sense of ownership of the dynamics of the call by using phrases such as "you earned a 4 on this" instead of "I gave you a 4 on this"?

| generating commitment | 4 | 3 | 2 | 1 | 0 |

As the session concludes, does the supervisor induce the rep to commit to specific objectives for maintaining strengths as well as reducing weaknesses?

Performance Evaluation: TEAMeasures

| scoring | 4 | 3 | 2 | 1 | 0 |

How accurate are the supervisor's numerical scores? Does she "double-dip" when scoring, deducting points twice for the same scorable event?

| inclusion | 4 | 3 | 2 | 1 | 0 |

Are the TEAMeasures definitions inserted with appropriate frequency to promote understanding of the scoring system and its application to the call?

| interpretation | 4 | 3 | 2 | 1 | 0 |

Does the supervisor identify all scorable events in the conversation? Are the appropriate defined categories applied to the call?

| use of tape | 4 | 3 | 2 | 1 | 0 |

Does the supervisor use audiotape with sufficient frequency to provide support for her evaluations? Is the tape rewound and replayed when a point is in doubt, or when repetition would promote understanding?

Informal Coaching and Counseling

| time management | 4 | 3 | 2 | 1 | 0 |

How effectively does the supervisor use his time when he is in the phone environment? Is he able to accurately detect and describe group performance within a few minutes of unobtrusive listening to one side of calls when in the room—that is, when he is overhearing the rep's conversation instead of being plugged into the call via an extension? Can he provide effective feedback after plugging into one complete call?

energy   4   3   2   1   0

How enthusiastic is the supervisor when in the phone environment?

communication   4   3   2   1   0
climate

How positive are the relations between the supervisor and reps on the supervisor's team? Do they welcome her input? How comfortable are the reps when she is present? How open are they to her criticism? Do reps on the team willingly offer help to one another?

proportionality   4   3   2   1   0

How does the supervisor balance his input with respect to the communications versus technical aspects of the rep's performance?

Scoring: Possible Points   =   (64)
                     Points Earned   =
                     Percentage of Effectiveness   =
                     (multiply points earned by 1.5625)

Improvement Objectives:
(1)
(2)
(3)
(4)
(5)

Manager's Summary:

Supervisor's Response:

_____   _____

Supervisor's Signature   *Manager's Signature*

EFFECTIVE CUSTOMER SERVICE MANAGEMENT PRACTICES

The SEAmeasures system operates from the premise that effective managers, supervisors, and team leaders perform no fewer than 16 vital practices that help them to succeed. I'm going to summarize these practices in a series of proactive statements and then plug them into the SEAmeasures instrument. (When I use the term "managers," I'm generally referring to team leaders and supervisors, as well. I assume that all three engage in coaching and counseling of reps and/or of fellow managers.)

(1) Managers organize the coaching and counseling session in an efficient way. They should begin by providing an overview of what will be covered in the session. They should also mention the sequence in which the topics will be covered. By doing this right away, they establish their credibility. They also create a comfortable atmosphere for the rep, who can track the progress he's making as the discussion ensues.

The manager must adhere to her announced structure and not deviate. If she fails to follow her own structure, she'll lose credibility, and she'll arouse uncertainty and insecurity in the rep.

The ability to get the session off on a good footing and maintain its structure is captured in the first SEAmeasures scale: Organization. Again, here is the definition:

organization 　　　　　4　　　3　　　2　　　1　　　0

Does the supervisor provide an overview at the beginning of the session? Does his commentary follow an announced pattern (that is, Call Path elements first, then customer response, then speech characteristics)?

(2) Managers should involve reps in coaching sessions by actively seeking their participation. According to behavioral scientists, we aren't persuaded by other people nearly as often, or as well, as when we're persuaded by ourselves. Another way of saying this is to note that people can talk themselves into or out of nearly anything and feel quite comfortable about it as long as they feel they've freely chosen the outcome.

By motivating reps to participate fully in the coaching and counseling session, we facilitate the self-persuasion process. We want reps to arrive at a number of realizations.

First, we want them to appreciate the usefulness of the Call Path and TEAMeasures systems. They should hear "proof" as the session proceeds that these tools really work to engineer enhanced service for the customer.

We also want them to know that we're acting in good faith. One of our main goals is to produce fair and meaningful evaluations. By involving reps in their own evaluation process, we're sending an important message of openness. At the same time, by asking them to share their input, we're creating several opportunities for them to come to grips with the challenge of changing their habits.

A good session enables them to grumble a little and let off steam. They can also hear solid answers to their questions about the new service practices. In this way, they can debunk certain misconceptions. This frees them to inject their energy into implementing change, instead of fighting it.

Our Evaluation Systems Should Involve Participative Decision Making (PDM)

Over the years a lot has been said and written about PDM (Participative Decision Making). The entire concept is that people should participate in making decisions that affect them; thus, they'll feel better about executing their "marching orders," because they will have had a hand in fashioning them.

Our coaching and counseling sessions operate in a manner that's consistent with this principle. What we don't want is a manager who dominates the session with his ideas about what the rep did, or how well she did it. Interactions need to be balanced, nearly 50/50, with the manager's and the rep's views. So, the second SEAmeasures scale is Participation.

participation   4   3   2   1   0

Does the supervisor balance the session with his perceptions as well as use questions properly to involve the rep?

(3) Managers need to use positive nonverbal communications to create a supportive atmosphere for evaluation and improvement. We know that body language and vocal tones mean a great deal in creating certain impressions in people. Managers should carefully "manage" these impressions during the coaching session. Specifically, they should show positive regard for reps by smiling. If they look too serious, they could easily "de-skill" their people, while seeming unduly punitive.

Managers should also make frequent eye contact with reps. Studies have shown that people who are given eye contact develop more positive regard for the "lookers" than for those who focus their attention elsewhere. Making eye contact also tends to send a message of sincerity that says the manager is honest and forthright.

There are some exceptions to using a lot of eye contact. When offering corrective criticism, especially when covering a point that has been previously covered, it helps to look at the tape recorder. That way, we take the sting out of our feedback. By the same token, when offering praise, directly looking into the rep's eyes can reinforce her feelings of achievement for something well done.

A positive vocal tone is communicated when managers make their voices "crest," as we've described it in the TEAMeasures definition of General Demeanor/Cheerfulness. Coaching and counseling sessions should be kept as "light" as possible; when offering correction, managers should express a tone that says, "But you can fix this very easily!"

I should also point out that certain environments are more conducive to coaching and counseling. Sitting at a round table is probably optimal, because this distributes the power among participants. If there is no "head" of the table, this facilitates a freer flow of ideas and opinions.

If you use a square or rectangular table, try to sit "around the corner" of a table with the rep. This simulates a side-by-side orientation. The worst seating arrangement is where the manager is "squared-off" against the rep, across the divide of a table. This can exaggerate perceived differences in opinion, make the setting of objectives a less cooperative endeavor, and create an unfriendly tone.

The third SEAmeasures scale captures these considerations. It is Nonverbal Communication.

nonverbal	4	3	2	1	0
communication					

Does the supervisor use body and facial expressions as well as vocal tone to create a positive atmosphere for rep evaluation?

(4) Managers should provide reps with high-grade, balanced feedback. We learn the most from what is called high-grade criticism. This is feedback that not only tells us that we did something well or not well but that also explains how we did it, possibly why we did it, and its effect. For example, a manager might say:

"That's a perfect Promise of Help that you inserted!" If she said no more than this, it would be considered low-grade criticism. The word "perfect" is indeed pleasant to hear, and it conveys the idea that we couldn't have done it any better. However, although this comment will inflate the rep's ego, it doesn't tell her exactly what she did, why it's important, and what its effects are. Here is what high-grade criticism sounds like:

"That's a perfect Promise of Help that you inserted! First, you earned all of your points for this Call Path segment because you said, 'Sure, I'll be happy to help you with that.' You also used the right tone, because the word, 'that,' is the highest word in the phrase. So, you're earning all of your Pitch points.

"Your Timing was also perfect because you inserted it immediately after the customer asked, 'Do you deliver on Saturdays?' That's just when you want to insert it, right after a question has been asked or a statement has been made. And you may have noticed that all of your work paid off right away, because what did the customer say, right after you did the Promise of Help?"

("Oh, great!"?)

"That's right. What does that mean, when a customer says 'Oh, great,' at that point?"

("That she's relieved and happy that she's going to get the help she called for.")

"Exactly. You did that perfectly. Let's replay the tape to hear it, again."

This would constitute high-grade criticism. You might be thinking, "That's a little long-winded, isn't it?" It seems so, especially when compared to the low-grade variety, but it serves a very important reinforcement function. By explaining fully, the manager reinforces the necessity of, and the benefits derived from, using the Call Path.

Did you notice in this excerpt that the manager created participation by asking questions of the rep about the effect of a perfectly executed Promise of Help? These questions involve the rep in the counseling process, which is one of the SEAmeasures concepts.

One more aspect of this SEAmeasure is pertinent. Over the course of the coaching and counseling session, managers should try to balance their criticism, so they don't unduly and relentlessly "slam" their reps with negatives. Managers tend to give too much weight to reps' weaknesses. We want to avoid this by forcing ourselves to find strengths as well.

So, our fourth SEAmeasures scale pertains to Feedback.

feedback		4	3	2	1	0

Does the supervisor provide high-grade criticism that emphasizes not only what was positive or negative but also explains the significance of the criticism to the rest of the conversation? Or does the supervisor merely announce what he likes or dislikes without explaining effects on the customer or the company? Does the supervisor balance his criticism by identifying strengths as well as weaknesses in the rep's performance?

(5) Managers should communicate ambitious but realistic performance standards for individual reps as well as for the entire customer service team. As you know, excellence in customer service isn't an accident. It results from setting and achieving ambitious goals. Everyone benefits from being continuously challenged, and the measurement systems you're learning in this book enable managers and reps to quantify their goals with great precision.

I'm sure you'd agree that it is realistic and meaningful for a rep to say, "I'm going to earn all 16 available points on the Call Path segment of TEAMeasures, and I'm going to earn them by doing the Call Path, word-for-word." That's a crystal-clear goal statement, isn't it? But what if we didn't employ TEAMeasures? What achievements could a rep commit to? "I'm going to try to provide better service"? That's nice but terribly imprecise.

Managers have a great opportunity within coaching and counseling sessions to say, "We're shooting for a team average of 90% on our TEAMeasures scores, which means you should be shooting for 90% or higher, okay?" By helping reps to set their sights on the proper target, managers are much more likely to meet their objectives. By the end of each coaching session, the manager and the rep are going to set specific objectives for the rep to pursue in order to maintain strengths and to improve weaknesses.

When managers articulate and reiterate performance standards, this makes the objective-setting process smooth and meaningful. So, the fifth SEAmeasures scale is Establishing Standards.

establishing standards		4	3	2	1	0

To what extent are group/individual goals for performance made known to the rep? Is the rep made aware of existing as well as targeted group averages on the TEAMeasures scale?

(6) Managers need to communicate clearly and understandably. Managers who use the systems presented in this book appreciate that they don't have to "invent" their criticism with each coaching and counseling session they conduct. "Good customer service" has already been predefined for them through the Call Path and the TEAMeasures systems. Therefore, they can speak with precision and avoid confusing reps.

Managers err when they casually substitute lay terms, or their own classifications, for established TEAMeasures categories. For example, a manager would really muddy the conversational waters if she said: "You really sound enthusiastic, there."

"Enthusiasm" isn't a TEAMeasures category, so a rep can't know what behaviors to repeat in order to sound enthusiastic again. TEAMeasures' category is General Demeanor/Cheerfulness. This is what should be used.

Therefore, our sixth SEAmeasures category is Creating Clarity.

creating   4   3   2   1   0
  clarity

Does the supervisor use simple, clear, and unambiguous language to explain points and to elucidate principles?

(7) Managers should encourage reps to take responsibility for their achievements. The taking of personal responsibility for one's performance is a crucial requirement for promoting effective service and the growth of our reps and fellow managers. *Fundamentally, the entire TEAMeasures and Call Path systems operate on one major assumption: that the rep is the primary agent in charge of causing call outcomes. We're saying that our reps are the masters of their communications and the architects of the results they obtain with customers.*

We shouldn't accept excuses or alibis, or offer sympathy if reps fail because they haven't followed directions. Providing they have been instructed well and managed appropriately, they should know precisely what to do; when to do it; and how to do it. Then it's their responsibility to perform properly. Therefore, in our coaching sessions we're not going to put up with, let alone promote, the shifting of responsibility from the rep to the customer, to environmental or extraneous factors, or to management.

Case in Point: Shirley was having difficulty coaching and counseling her reps. They constantly questioned why she "gave" them various scores. A videotape of one of her coaching sessions revealed the reason.

Shirley got into trouble because she repeatedly used the phrase, "I gave you a 2 on . . ." a given measure. Instead, as we have seen, she should have been promoting responsibility in reps for their results. A more appropriate phrase is "You earned a 2 on calibration." Responsibility-promoting phraseology makes it clear that TEAMeasures scores are created by the rep and are not simply "gifts" or penalties arbitrarily assigned by the manager.

By repeating responsible phrasing, managers reduce the tendency among some reps to make excuses. Typical excuses include "The customer wouldn't let me get the Promise of Help in" and "The client was already mad when she called, and I couldn't do anything about it."

I'm not saying you'll never hear these claims if you use responsibility-promoting language. Yet, I can assure you that alibis and excuses of this type will be much less prevalent. That'll save you time, reduce conflict, increase compliance, and accelerate positive customer outcomes. Moreover, it will assist reps to mature as people, because they'll accept responsibility for themselves, as well as their behaviors and their consequences. So, the seventh SEAmeasure is Promoting Responsibility.

promoting responsibility	4	3	2	1	0

Does the supervisor instill a sense of ownership of the dynamics of the call by using phrases such as "You earned a 4 on this" instead of "I gave you a 4 on this"?

(8) Effective managers get reps to commit to fulfilling specific performance objectives. The worst of all possible coaching and counseling scenarios is one in which reps listen silently to their managers' feedback, nod their heads in agreement, leave the session, and then don't change any of the behaviors that were discussed. This happens much of the time in programs that don't fully use the TEAMeasures and SEAmeasures philosophy.

Central to our philosophy is the practice of having reps score their own calls, in addition to having their managers score the same calls. This strategy gets reps involved in their own achievement, while providing an incentive to set and follow specific objectives for improvement.

Administratively, it would seem much more "convenient" to just have managers do the scoring. Then, they could just dash through the sessions, while *telling* reps how they scored. But this would rob reps of the chance to internalize the process. It would also take away the feeling of "ownership" that reps who self-score obtain.

Being scored without scoring themselves also denies reps a deeper understanding of how calls really operate to create certain effects. By actively participating in the scoring process, reps gain the knowledge to make accurate and responsible judgments about the quality of their work. This knowledge guides them on a day-to-day basis, between formal measurement periods. Thus managers have to do less overt supervision, because reps have internalized high-quality standards and could be said to be essentially supervising themselves.

By the time a coaching and counseling session is winding down, the rep should have a clear idea of her strengths and weaknesses and should be willing to set objectives for maintaining strengths and for making corrections. To be effective, goals and objectives need to be explicit, written down, agreed to by all parties, and frequently tracked for progress in their attainment.

So, effective managers get their reps to commit to certain specific performance objectives. We measure this capability to produce consensus under the category Generating Commitment.

generating commitment	4	3	2	1	0

Does the supervisor induce the rep to commit to specific objectives for maintaining strengths as well as reducing weaknesses as the session draws to a conclusion?

The following four SEAmeasures evaluate the manager's ability to use the TEAMeasures system in the coaching and counseling context.

(9) Managers need to accurately score conversations. The ideal system for training managers to measure customer service performance capabilities consists of two steps. First, managers should attend seminars that explain the Call Path, TEAMeasures, and SEAmeasures systems. They need to read all definitions and practice scoring sample calls from other companies.

By focusing on other companies' calls they can be objective, and there's no reason to be anything but thorough and rigorous in their assessments. If they were scoring their own calls, at least right away, they would tend to pull their punches.

Within the seminars, participating managers should also view videotapes of managers from other companies who are performing coaching and counseling functions. SEAmeasures scales are used to evaluate the performances of the managers who appear on videotape. This gives trainee-managers experience in using SEAmeasures in a low-threat setting, before they engage in self-scoring.

After attending seminars, managers move into the second step of their training. They are coached on an individual basis. During this period, they score some of their own reps, and they then coach and counsel those reps. Sessions are videotaped, and managers view their videos and score themselves, using SEAmeasures.

A trainer, or one of his managers, views and scores the same videotaped sessions. Then the trainer and each manager get together, review the video, and discuss their scores. They set new performance objectives for the critiqued manager. Here is the SEAmeasures category for capturing the manager's TEAMeasures scoring capability:

scoring	4	3	2	1	0

How accurate are the supervisor's numerical scores? Does she "double-dip" when scoring, deducting points twice for the same scorable event?

(10) During coaching sessions, managers need to frequently refer to the TEAMeasures definitions in order to perform proper scoring and to promote universal understanding of the system. As you know, people learn through reinforcements and rewards. Essential to promoting the learning process is making sure reps and managers apply the proper evaluative criteria to calls. They're taught to do so by repeatedly reading the TEAMeasures definitions, together, as the coaching and counseling session proceeds.

Example: When covering a call with his rep, Bill felt that a point should have been deducted for inserting the Promise of Help too late in the conversation.

Bill said: "Paul, I think you could have inserted the Promise of Help earlier— right after the customer said 'I have a problem with my computer.' Let's see where that would be scored in the TEAMeasures system. I think we can find it under Calibration. Let's read this together. Here it is:

"'A late insertion of a part of the Call Path is a Calibration problem, as well.' So, let's make sure we deduct one point from Calibration, okay?"

How well did Bill do in inserting TEAMeasures definitions?

Bill would have been much less effective if he had simply said, "You're late bringing in the Promise of Help, so let's deduct a point from Calibration, okay?" By repeating the definition, he lends immediate authority to the score, while reinforcing the definition in his mind, as well as in his rep's mind.

This practice is captured under the SEAmeasures definition of Inclusion:

inclusion   4   3   2   1   0

Are the TEAMeasures definitions inserted with appropriate frequency to promote understanding of the scoring system and its application to the call?

(11) Managers need to identify all scorable events in conversations while applying the appropriate definition categories to them. It takes a lot of concentration and thoroughness for a manager to perform properly in the role of coach and counselor. She must be able to spot scorable events. This means her antennae need to be constantly tuned to the nuances of text, tone, and timing. She also needs to be willing to confront reps with their mistakes, as well as be prepared to praise them when they do well.

Many managers don't enjoy being put into the role of being a "drill sergeant," but this is akin to what they become, to some degree, when they coach and counsel. They need to capture and correct *all* the errors that reps make. Otherwise, reps will receive inconsistent instruction, while processing a message that tells them that "almost" or "sometimes correct" is good enough. (Remember: Drill sergeants are appreciated, at long last, when their trainees know exactly what to do and then do it well, under all conditions.)

Thoroughness is one goal for the manager, but she must also strive to apply the appropriate definition criteria to the scorable events she identifies.

Example: Your rep snaps at a customer: "Hold on for a second, won't you?" Which TEAMeasures definition(s) should you and your rep apply to this scorable event? There isn't an obvious answer to this one. But it is discourteous, isn't it? The definition of Courtesy tells us that it is the "frequent use of 'please' and 'thank-you.'" Would a "please" have helped this phrase? I think it would have, if it had prefaced the comment: "Please hold on for a second, won't you?"

But there is a second definition that could apply—the one that deals with Empathy/Supportiveness. Under Defensiveness, we see that messages that are brusque and "controlling" should be avoided. The command made to the customer to "Hold on for a second, won't you?" could sound defensive and abrupt.

So, the manager and the rep need to read through both definitions and replay the offensive language until they believe they have chosen the proper definition. It could be that Courtesy is the better scale to score, because it tells a rep what to do, on a proactive basis, in the future.

Our instruction to the rep would be to "Use 'Please' with greater frequency, especially when asking a customer to hold the line." By selecting the proper definition, the manager will be fulfilling the requirements of the SEAmeasure pertaining to Interpretation:

interpretation   4   3   2   1   0

Does the supervisor identify all scorable events in the conversation? Are the appropriate definitional categories applied to the call?

(12) During the coaching session, managers should frequently play and replay various segments of the call. As you know, a major goal of the systems we're employing is to be objective. We want to take coaching and counseling out of the arena of subjective opinion and bring it into the realm of objectivity.

When we're using tapes of actual calls, we have a clear record of what transpired in given transactions. But because we've heard a tape only once, we shouldn't delude ourselves into thinking that we've accurately or thoroughly heard what's there.

In fact, certain TEAMeasures definitions come to life only after we have replayed portions of the tape several times. This is especially apparent when we're scoring a customer's tone. Usually, it takes three to five repetitions of the tape of the end of the call to hear, with clarity, how much a customer "sang."

An equally important function that is served by playing the tape is proving to the rep that a scorable event occurred.

Example: Supervisor Bill is coaching Merilee about her use of the Call Path. He says: "Great, you did the Greeting word-for-word, so you earned all four points. But I think your speed was too fast, so you lost a point there. Let's look at the next part of the Call Path, the Promise of Help . . ."

If you were Merilee, what would you think of Bill's statement that he "thinks your speed was too fast"? How credible was Bill's comment, without an offering of proof? If he said that to me, I'd probably say, "Really? Let's hear the tape, again."

Fortunately, Bill and the rep don't have to stop at this point. The TEAMeasures definition of Speed contains an objective standard that should be applied. It says that a rep's word speed is too slow if it falls below 100 words per minute. It is too fast if it exceeds 150 words per minute.

Bill and Merilee can compute her speed, with precision. Her Greeting is where she supposedly exceeded the upper range of the speed limit. So, all they need to do is replay the tape of the Greeting. Then, using a watch with a second hand, they can calculate how much time it takes for her to utter the entire greeting.

Let's assume that the Greeting contains 13 words. If Merilee got through it in 6 seconds, she is speaking at a rate of 130 words per minute. That is neither too slow nor too fast. In fact, it is just right! By replaying the tape, and by making the proper calculation, Bill can judge this and score Speed objectively and correctly.

Why should he or Merilee settle for his impression that he "thinks" she exceeded the speed limit, when they can know with certainty whether she did or didn't?

By using the tape at proper intervals, the manager simply does his job much better. This SEAmeasures performance dimension is scored under the heading of Use of Tape:

| use of tape | 4 | 3 | 2 | 1 | 0 |

Does the supervisor use audiotape with sufficient frequency to provide support for her evaluations? Is the tape rewound and replayed when a point is in doubt, or when repetition would promote understanding?

The final four SEAmeasures categories apply to how the manager performs during Informal Coaching and Counseling. This occurs outside the formal sessions that involve the scoring of a rep's calls. Usually, Informal Coaching and Counseling happens deskside and within the more public environment of the CSR workroom.

Here, we're concerned with evaluating what we discussed earlier as "managing by walking around"—that is, how a manager performs "on the fly," as she "patrols" the service environment.

(13) Managers should be able to walk through the CSR workroom and quickly hear and evaluate how numerous reps are performing. In part, I refer to this managerial capability as "stereoscopic listening." It is like "aiming one's ears" in several directions at once, to assess the use of the Call Path and related performance. By being able to do this, managers can quickly praise or correct rep practices between formal measurement periods.

Recommended Procedure: When I'm training managers, as part of their individualized coaching and counseling, I'll walk through the customer service center. I'll whisper these questions to them:

Can you tell me who is using the Call Path and who isn't?
Who is stair-stepping with their tone?
Who is using the right timing?

What else do you think you can quickly detect by using the practice of managing by walking around? When managers use MBWA, they can obtain an instant "snapshot" of what their people are doing and how they're doing it. By doing this, they'll be utilizing their time very well.

But there's another element to being able to manage one's time well, and that is being able to succinctly critique reps as one listens to calls within the working environment. This occurs when the manager sits next to the rep, listens to a conversation, and then "casually" comments on the prominent features of the interaction he heard.

Example: A manager could easily provide this sort of quick feedback:

"Nice work, Jerry. You were on the Call Path, word for word, and your pitch moved up nicely, just as it should have. But I did have a question about the timing you used in inserting the Promise of Help. Could you have put it into the conversation earlier? You know, immediately following the customer's question?"

("I guess so.")

"Try to do that, because it'll shorten the call and put the customer at ease much faster, okay? Otherwise, you're sounding great! Good job."

How much time would this quick feedback session take? A few minutes? Add this onto a 3-minute call, and the manager would need to invest only 5–7 minutes in a quick, informal coaching and counseling session.

But within that time, the rep could get clear and meaningful feedback, and the manager could hear exactly what's being said and sense how one of her teammates is doing. This sort of quick interaction also is significant because the rep can't help but appreciate that the manager is taking time with her, and that she cares about the quality of her unit.

So, there are payoffs all around when managers "patrol" and coach in this manner. Here is the pertinent SEAmeasure that captures this process:

time		4	3	2	1	0
management						

How effectively does the supervisor use her time when she is within the phone environment? Is she able to accurately detect and describe group performance within a few minutes of unobtrusive listening to one side of calls when in the room? Can she provide effective feedback after "plugging-into" one complete call?

(14) Managers should express enthusiasm and inject energy into the workroom. When I was a mere pup, I worked with a dynamo by the name of Larry. He was Time/Life Books' general manager in Santa Monica, California. He founded the telephone circulation division of that company, and he was a mentor who taught me a great deal about the power of enthusiasm.

When Larry entered the work area, he'd light up. Yes, he may have been totally serious a moment before, in the privacy of his office, but the moment he emerged from his solitude, he was "on stage."

"How ya doing?" he'd bellow, even if you were only 18 inches away. If you didn't respond with, "Great, Larry!" or something equally robust, he'd repeat his question, with a puzzled expression on his face, and with even more energy.

Do you think you could do something similar to inject energy into the service center?

Larry's electricity was simply irresistible. Nobody could keep a frown or even a neutral expression on his face when Larry lit up like this. Instantly, we knew that great results were expected from us and that we had better not kick back and "cruise" during our shifts.

Larry was serving as an excellent role model by being so energetic. We got a charge from his voltage, and he got a charge back from us. Everyone prospered, and the time flew by.

Larry simply wouldn't accept anything but outstanding morale in his work unit. If someone was down in the dumps, Larry would recommend this course of action: "Go outside for five minutes. Then come back in with a smile on your face, okay?"

Managers set the tone for their associates. Make sure it's an energetic, enthusiastic one, and you'll earn your SEAmeasures points on this scale:

energy 4 3 2 1 0

How enthusiastic is the supervisor when he is in the phone environment?

(15) Managers need to create an open communication climate in the service center. I realize that we're introducing a challenging system for monitoring, measuring, and managing service work. Right now, it may seem that the mood in the workroom could be a ponderous one as you implement these new routines. And, if you don't take precautions, it could become a defensive environment because we are critiquing our associates on a continuous basis. But it's the manager's job to make sure that a supportive atmosphere is created.

We want to create an atmosphere in which people feel that they're accepting feedback for their own betterment, so that they can achieve more, for customers, for their company, and for themselves.

What do you think managers can do to assure that the communications climate will remain open and constructive?

Managers can develop an open communications climate by using positive nonverbal communications, just as they should in coaching sessions. Smiling a great deal really helps! It doesn't matter if you don't feel like smiling. Try to do it, anyway.

One of my earliest public speaking teachers was one of Dale Carnegie's original instructors. He said: "I'll take an insincere smile any day, over a sincere frown!" For years, I questioned the wisdom of this remark. Wasn't "putting on a happy face" dishonest if you didn't feel like doing it? Shouldn't you wear your emotions on your sleeve, no matter how positive or negative they are?

At least, that was what I used to wonder, but now I see what my venerable professor meant. It is a leader's responsibility to manage the moods in her work group and to lead by example. This task is fulfilled by subordinating her private feelings in the interest of the greater good of promoting the positive feelings of others.

Troops that are being sent into combat don't have focus groups about their fears. They learn to control these feelings while generating the bravado that will help them, and their associates, to get through the difficulties to come. They act boldly, despite their fears and personal misgivings. They smile when events could make them dour.

So, a positive communications climate is created partly through constructive nonverbal displays. There are some other things you can do to maintain an open atmosphere. Show your good will toward reps by making sure to follow a negative or corrective criticism with a positive statement of some sort. Get into the habit of tagging each correction with one of these kinds of statements:

But you're sounding good, overall . . .
By changing this, you'll get the sort of customer response you really deserve, which is a positive one . . .
But you're making great progress. Your Call Path is excellent.

Here is the SEAmeasure that applies to creating an open communications climate:

communications climate	4	3	2	1	0

How positive are the relations between the supervisor and reps on the supervisor's team? Do they welcome her input? How comfortable are they when she is present? How open are they to her criticism? Do reps on the team willingly offer help to one another?

(16) Managers should use informal coaching and counseling to improve the "technical" performance of their CSRs. CSRs are evaluated not only for their communicative achievements but also for their delivery of company "content." This is the informational component of their work, and it is captured on the TEAMeasures scoring sheet under the heading Explanations.

For reps to perform well, they need to be instructed, and instruction should occur not only in formal classes but also informally, in the workroom. As managers critique the use of the Call Path they can easily augment the knowledge of their reps, as they hear customers raise various questions and issues.

The final SEAmeasures category, Proportionality, assesses the manager's ability to provide both communications- and content-related feedback to reps. Here's how we define it:

proportionality   4   3   2   1   0

How does the supervisor balance her input with respect to the communications versus technical aspects of the rep's performance?

Increasingly, service personnel are being asked to perform at least limited marketing duties, so, in the next chapter, we'll see what it takes to help them do this. We'll also try to define a potential career path that reps can follow to develop their full potential. Thus, we'll turn our attention to recruiting, motivating, and retaining quality customer service people. We'll look into what is referred to as a "Service IQ," and we'll also discuss methods for compensating and motivating reps.

Recruiting, Motivating, and Retaining Quality Customer Service People

In a free and mobile society we can be assured of one fact: We'll never have a monopoly on recruiting and retaining the best employees. Additionally, "all of us make hiring mistakes," according to management guru, Peter Drucker. Nonetheless, there are several practices that we can introduce into our organizations that should make our companies more attractive to work for and much harder for quality people to leave.

In this chapter we're going to identify these practices by focusing on these questions:

- What is the profile of an exceptional CSR?
- How can we recruit these individuals?
- How should we motivate them and compensate them?
- What "tricks" do the most successful firms use to retain their top-notch people?
- How can we create challenging and rewarding career paths for these individuals?

A PROFILE OF EXCEPTIONAL CSRS

Some people seem to be born with a service aptitude, or high "Service I.Q." They intuitively sense what customers need to know and hear, and they consistently deliver it. You might call these folks "natural-born CSRs," just in the same way that some people are called "naturals" in other areas, such as sales.

If you study the attributes of these naturals, you'll find that they possess several attributes that we can build into a recruiting model. Although we know that we can "make" nearly anyone into an effective customer service representative by using the techniques presented in this book, why not boost our odds of developing a first class team by finding people who are also naturally suited to the work?

One of the essential qualities of exceptional CSRs is their *desire to help other people.* They are drawn to an occupation like service in the same way that many people are attracted to teaching and medicine. This is to say that great CSRs are *people-oriented people.* They have a high need for social interaction in their jobs. Generally, this means they're much more outgoing and extroverted than clerical personnel. A living hell for gifted CSRs would be having to work on a task all by themselves, day after day, with no end in sight.

For exceptional CSR candidates, being a member of a team is much more than an abstract concept or a slogan. They enjoy being interdependent; that is, they take comfort in the fact that they can depend on others. They also feel a sense of pride in the fact that they, in turn, can be relied on by their peers.

Many of the people who are selected to work for Disneyland and Disney World embody this kind of "team" attitude. In fact, they are urged to see themselves as part of "The Cast." Their number-one job is to show patrons a good time, and they do it by thinking of themselves as integral parts of the performance, even if their jobs place them far from an official "stage."

Excellent CSRs are also *talkers.* Most of them really enjoy communicating by phone. Contrast them with those who suffer from what I call "phone fear." Phone fear is a form of situational shyness that prevents people from comfortably interacting with others. While phone-shy people can be taught to overcome this problem, they are not good candidates to perform phone work.

I suggest you ask CSR candidates how they feel about handling 100 calls per day, for example. If they wince, or seem hesitant to say they wouldn't mind, they might not be suited for this type of work.

Excellent CSRs really *love to stay busy.* They don't mind handling numerous transactions, providing that they have the time to give them their best effort. *They also enjoy meeting the challenges of their work that mediocre candidates would find highly unattractive.* For instance, one senior service manager I worked with in a mutual fund company said she takes delight in handling very angry customers. She said it is exhilarating when she can turn them around in a single call and have them thank her and sound pleased before the conversation concludes.

I think you'll find that the people who are the top performers at any job reflect the same sort of zeal about their work. They are often so absorbed in their assignments that they forget about the clock.

Excellent CSRs are able to emotionally identify with their employers as well as their clients. We have all had the experience of dealing with CSRs who aren't able to accomplish this balancing act. They err by coming across to clients as if they're guarding their own, personal fortress.

Good reps realize that they're professional go-betweens. They feel a duty to their employer and to customers, but, instead of going overboard in identifying with the concerns of one or the other, they're able to bring balance and a spirit of equity to both. This takes a certain amount of diplomacy to accomplish, which leads us to the next attribute. *Successful CSRs are able to get along with different sorts of people from diverse backgrounds. In a sense, they have the ability to please most of the people, most of the time.*

Example: I was chosen to be part of an elite training team recruited by the U.S. Navy to deliver the largest civilian management training program in history. Our mission was to train 18,000 senior-level navy managers within 18 months. Specifically, we needed to elicit the cooperation of our trainees in implementing the Civil Service Reform Act. The Act called for managers to be paid not only for the time they worked on the job (seniority) but also based on their effectiveness.

This Merit-Pay Program was controversial, and a large proportion of trainees were openly antagonistic. Our assignment was to overcome their resistance and to encourage them to understand, support, and fully implement the program.

At the end of each class, written evaluations were collected from trainees. Despite their initial resistance, the great majority of participants scored their instructors as "excellent" and the course as "very good" to "excellent." In short, our performance exceeded all expectations.

How did we pull it off?

Despite adversarial circumstances, we proved that you can come very close to pleasing the great majority of customers all of the time. It takes special care and unique skills, but it can be done.

Here is our secret. As trainers, we were provided with first-class instruction in how to teach resistant people. This enabled us to perceive the resistance as normal and as an achievable challenge to overcome. We learned to see resistance in new ways, not just as a show-stopping impediment.

Set your standards high when you're recruiting. Tell your new reps that you are trying to please all of the people all of the time. Make this your goal, and you'll probably come very close to achieving it—quite a challenging standard.

In addition, *prospective CSRs should be able to accept criticism in an agreeable, nondefensive manner.* This isn't easy if one is thin-skinned or if one fosters an inflated self-image. In fact, it is a mark of maturity when one can appreciate the feedback others offer, whether it's good or bad. For example, I acted as a speech consultant to a congressional candidate who won an election and then went on to serve several terms. One of his greatest assets was his ability to amiably accept, and then immediately implement, constructive criticism. When I coached him, he closed his eyes in an effort to visualize exactly what I was recommending. Then, he immediately acted on my suggestions. He didn't waste a second in fighting me or in ducking my advice. He realized that I was saying everything for his benefit, and he responded in kind. CSR candidates need to be capable of doing the same thing.

I suggest you ask potential hires this simple but powerful question: "How easily can you accept feedback and criticism?" This question should get their attention. By judging their first response, you'll probably recognize right away who is going to be defensive and who will constructively accept and act on your feedback. I've heard folks who can handle criticism respond with words such as these: "I played sports in school, and I've had to take a lot of criticism. I know it's for my own good, and the coach is there to help me to improve."

Defensive candidates are likely to try to duck the question or to provide a lukewarm reply, such as: "Gee, that's a good question. I don't know. I suppose if the criticism is said nicely, and it's not aimed at me personally, then it's all right." Also, highly achieving CSRs are usually pleased about their prior working experiences.

I've interviewed and hired hundreds of people, and my "trouble alarm" goes off when job candidates express hostility or dissatisfaction about a past employer or about a previous occupation. In many cases, these are folks who are running from something, instead of seeking something positive at your place of business.

Instead of "rescuing" these applicants from their unfortunate pasts, which is a temptation, you should instead look for individuals who perceive their experiences as being appropriate and helpful to their development. That's a constructive and healthy frame of mind, and if you choose people who think this way, you'll avoid some potentially "troubled" employees.

Great CSRs are often musically inclined. Musical ability can be a major predictor of success for a CSR. Musicians have a lot going for them that translates to service work. For instance, they're expert listeners. They can tune into customers' moods, and they can easily appreciate the various tones they need to produce to perform the Call Path and the Three Ts of Text, Tone, and Timing. They can also create rapport by intuitively echoing the tones they're hearing from customers. Most important, they can understand and respond quickly to subtle direction from management with respect to their telephone "performances."

Case in Point: One of the best communicators I ever recruited, trained, and managed was an aspiring jazz guitarist. He had a highly trained ability to "tune into" customers. In fact, I could hear him constantly adjusting his vocal tones to appeal to different customers. He knew the Call Path so well that he could do it word for word, close his eyes and simply concentrate on the breathing and vocal patterns of the prospect. By doing so, he intuitively grasped how to communicate a standard presentation in hundreds of customized ways.

Try This Experiment: Write down the names of your best CSRs. Then, casually ask them whether they sing, play an instrument, or consider themselves to be musical, in any way. My hunch is that you'll discover that some of your best reps are also quite musical.

Excellent CSR candidates are often "stakeholders" in the community. In other words, they're already "rooted," or they're seeking to put down roots. We live in a highly mobile and, some might say, a nearly nomadic society. People move around quite a bit, so you can't expect everyone to have grown up in and remained in their original neighborhoods. But some individuals are more rooted than others. Even if they hail from another state or nation, they're what can be called "stakeholders." They put down roots because they intend to stick around for a considerable period of time. They join organizations such as the PTA, and they support community activities. They take pride in the fact that they've had the same home address or telephone number for years.

Why would we be interested in these people? For one thing, we're going to be making quite an investment in their training, so the last thing we want to be is a bus stop on their journey to somewhere else.

Case in Point: One of my clients performs customer service and technical support for researchers in the biotechnology sector, and it takes at least six months for a rep to get up to speed on the products listed in the company's catalog. To complicate matters, just when reps have a grasp of the current inventory, "the products become obsolete, and reps have to be re-trained." So, the company is financially "upside down" for a long time as it invests in the development and educational updating of its personnel. It will start profiting from its efforts only if reps stick around for three or more years. Therefore, the company simply must recruit rooted people.

I wouldn't hesitate to ask employment candidates how long they expect to live in the area. By asking this question, you'll be diminishing CSR turnover—before it has a chance to begin!

Let's summarize the attributes of exceptional CSRs before we discuss how to attract them.

- They enjoy helping other people
- They are team players.
- They enjoy interacting with other people.
- They are talkers who like to communicate over the telephone.
- They like to stay busy with a full workload.
- They enjoy the specific challenges of customer service work—that is, conflict management.
- They enjoy becoming totally absorbed in their work.
- They're able to identify well with the company and the customers.
- They're diplomatic and able to get along with a wide range of personalities and people from diverse backgrounds.

- They accept feedback and criticism in a constructive way.
- They're generally pleased about their work experiences and about past employers.
- They're often musically inclined.
- They're stakeholders and "rooted" people.

RECRUITING GREAT REPS

Traditional Recruiting Methods

When recruiting, we should use traditional and nontraditional methods. Traditional methods include:

- Classified ads in newspapers and trade journals
- Employment agencies and "headhunters"
- In-company searches for capable candidates currently located in other departments
- Job fairs

Let's discuss these traditional approaches before turning our attention to nontraditional ones.

Running Classified Ads

Classified ads have a number of advantages. Newspapers can have broad circulations, so a large number of folks will see your ad. But who are the people who examine the classifieds? Many are unemployed for one reason or another. Some are employed but are curious to see if the grass is greener elsewhere. And others are actually your current employees.

If you're looking for solid people who don't jump around from job to job, the classifieds may not be for you. Additionally, because of the broad reach of metropolitan papers, many of the readers will be located well beyond a reasonable commuting distance. Thus, you may want to advertise in the classifieds of your local papers. Circulation is small, but people who want to stay where they are will be attracted to your ad. They're more likely to be stakeholders who identify with their communities.

If the trade journals relevant to your field accept classified ads, this can be a boon. People who are committed to your industry will respond, and they'll often be skilled and motivated. You might also consider advertising in the local or regional publications of customer service associations.

Remember, advertising pays off, providing that the ads are read by the right people. But it can also be expensive and wasteful. Be sure to include in your ad as much as you can about the attributes of your ideal CSR.

Employment Agencies and Headhunters

Employment agencies and headhunters should be used in tight labor markets. They are professionals who are paid to supply you with the people you need, and their fees can be a bargain. However, if the labor market is filled with abundant talent, you may want to tap into it directly.

Tapping Existing Employees

Existing employees can be recruited from other departments, whenever you can get the green light to use this resource. Consider the advantages of these folks who are already on board: They know the company, its culture, traditions, and products and services; they're already on the payroll, so they have to be screened only slightly; and you can skip having to verify past employment and a number of other details.

You can check existing employees' effectiveness by checking with their current managers. You can also see how they get along with the rest of the team by interviewing their peers. Of course, they won't have to relocate or change their commuting pattern or adjust in a number of other ways, as they would if they went to work for another firm—so, they'll get up to speed quickly in their new roles.

Now that I've said this, I should caution you to still be careful in your screening of in-house candidates. Make sure that they have all the communications and phone skills that exceptional candidates possess. Accordingly, remember to put them through the same gauntlet that others have to run. Specifically, speak to them over the phone a number of times, and evaluate their voices and delivery. If they have a "split personality," whereby they're warm and wonderful face to face but cold and lifeless over the phone, reject their candidacy. I know this can be tough to do, especially when they have numerous friends and boosters in the firm, but it must be done.

Job Fairs

Job fairs have become a fixture in the recruiting world in recent years. They can be effective if they're well organized. The concept of the fair is simple and powerful. Hundreds, and possibly thousands of job seekers and career changers, are drawn to a free event at a conference or convention center. Scores of employers are there, trying to recruit quality people. Heavy advertising supports these events, which are usually promoted up to six weeks in advance.

The greatest strength of the fair is that employers can meet potential hires face to face. If there is interest, they can set a time, during the same event, to discuss opportunities further. By the time the event concludes, an employer will have met multiple candidates. This saves time as well as money.

The risk to the employer is that currently employed people will be underrepresented in the ranks of those present at the event. Many simply can't break away from their jobs to invest the better part of a day in that setting. Others will be concerned that their existing employers might spot them in the crowd.

Nontraditional Recruiting Methods

The best way to assure that you'll have a large pool of desirable job candidates is to draw them from different sources, including those that aren't being drained by other employers who are also actively recruiting.

Here are a few suggestions you may want to explore:

- Industry seminars and other educational venues
- Your vendors' workforces
- Venues that you frequent in your off-hours
- Active networking among business and social contacts
- Local college departments, professors, and alumni associations

Seminars and Educational Meetings

One of the great side benefits of attending industry-sponsored or public seminars is that we get to interact with people of similar interests, skills, and even attitudes. For instance, if you were to sign up for a class on Managing Customer Conflict, you'd inevitably run into CSRs who have been sent by their companies for the purpose of updating and augmenting their skills.

In a sense, if your intention is to recruit them, these people have been pre-screened for you. Let's say you meet someone from IBM or from Xerox. Generally, such a person has been put through rather rigorous screening processes simply to get aboard such blue-chip firms. If you strike up a relationship with this person, you can bet on the fact that he or she has been carefully trained.

Of course, there are exceptions. Some companies that once were praised for delivering first-rate service can degenerate without much public notice. For instance, I once encountered a number of poorly trained folks from a famous catalogue company; not only were their skills primitive, their attitudes were worse. So, it's okay to generalize, but, to be safe, update your knowledge about firms with supposedly superior service and personnel.

One final note about folks whom you meet at seminars: By seeing them in action—how they comment on points made in the program, as well as when they respond to questions—you can unobtrusively judge a number of things about them. How well do they *articulate*? Are they really *listening* to the lecturer and to their fellow participants? Are they *eager to learn*? Do they seem to be *extroverted*? Are they *people-oriented people*? Many of the key characteristics that we're seeking in candidates are obvious to us in educational settings. So, try to attend as many conferences and seminars as you can. And bring plenty of business cards!

Vendors' Workforces

My insurance agent was quite a nice fellow; he once rushed to my house to repair a broken water pipe when I was out of town on business. Sadly, he just retired, so my account was shifted to someone with whom I have had no prior relationship. Well, maybe it's not so sad that Jim decided to play golf full time. His secretary is a gem. She has run his whole operation for more than 20 years. A total self-starter, she doesn't have to be told to do anything. She seems to intuit exactly what to do and when to do it to make the greatest contribution to the agency. In a word, she's a complete pleasure to interact with.

I had wanted to hire her for about 20 years. However, I couldn't bring myself to make her a serious offer because I knew she was Jim's "everything," and they were a great team. But now, it's a different story. I'm going to find out if she'd like to join me in my consulting practice.

Keep your antennae up and receptive for potential hires who work for your vendors. By communicating with them as a customer, you have a great chance to determine how service-sensitive they really are. All you need to do is compliment them and ask, "Have you ever considered working for another firm?"

Be Alert in Your Off-Hours

One of the best reps I ever hired was a waitress at a restaurant where I was a "regular" for a number of years. I couldn't help but notice her enthusiasm and high energy level. She also seemed to be the best customer-pleaser in the place, and she appreciated the opportunity I provided for her. It was a step up in pay, and the hours were a lot better.

I'd pay special attention to folks who are working in hospitality-related venues, such as restaurants and hotels. In many cases, they enjoy working with the public, and, again, they have been prescreened to some extent for you by their current employers.

Don't forget tourist attractions, either. I'm located 10 minutes from Universal Studios and 45 minutes from Disneyland. These companies insist on recruiting outgoing, people-oriented people, so they're excellent hunting grounds for new associates. Even if you don't have such internationally known attractions in your town, you probably have museums, movie theaters, and other places where the public is served, right? Recruit there!

Business and Social Networking

Do you remember the movie *Six Degrees of Separation*? The theme was that any one of us is connected to everyone else on this planet, through only six contacts. In other words, each of us knows someone who knows someone who knows someone who knows someone who knows someone who knows the exact person we need to meet or want to meet. This, as you probably know, is the basis of social and business networking.

Let's say we want to recruit the best CSR in the world. How could we identify that person? We could begin by communicating with our best friend. We might ask that person: "When and where did you last experience the best customer service?" Once he answered, we could add: "And do you remember the name of the person who served you?"

If we asked these questions of a dozen people, I'll bet we'd develop a pool of 3–6 excellent job candidates. And what would happen when we contacted the CSR candidates? We'd ask if they were available; if they weren't, we would ask them whom they knew who delivers top-notch service.

Within a short time, we'd have more candidates than we could handle. But that's a good problem, right?

Professors, Departments, and Alumni Associations

Colleges and universities have their own job boards and placement services, but I'm not going to suggest that you use them. I've found that they are no more helpful in supplying good candidates than the classifieds in a big-city newspaper. The reason is that these entities are understaffed and not set up to learn anything about the job seekers who use their services.

I would prefer to steer you to specific faculty members at colleges and universities. Call them and ask them for the names of their best grads during the past five to ten years. Chances are pretty good that these grads, if they excelled under the guidance of certain faculty members, will have stayed in touch and can be located.

If faculty or departments are reluctant to divulge names or phone numbers, ask if they can contact the grads on your behalf. They can then alert these prospects to the opportunity you're offering, while telling them how to get in touch with you. Faculty and departments are often aware of grads who are conducting job searches and who are motivated to find a good place to apply their skills.

I'm reasonably active in various university alumni associations. These volunteer-run organizations can also be a source of great contacts who can guide you to excellent job seekers. So, remember the old school tie. It works.

MOTIVATING AND COMPENSATING CSRS

I'm a strong believer in the concept of pay-for-performance, which is also known as merit pay. This is a system whereby those who perform at peak levels receive peak pay, while those whose output is average receive average pay.

Historically, it has been difficult to dispense high rewards in customer service for two main reasons. First, it has been easier, from an administrative standpoint, to pay all people a flat salary or on an hourly basis. It is usually clear when someone has punched the time clock, so paying her for her presence is simple and seemingly objective and fair. Second, there have been few viable ways to measure the objective of service—that is, customer satisfaction—or to link such measurement with the training of specific reps. Now that we have TEAMeasures, we have a tool for defining customer satisfaction and for evaluating rep performance. So, now we can objectively link service events and reps' behaviors to monetary rewards.

The philosophy of merit pay is simple and, I think, equitable. If Bill consistently makes customers sing, and they robustly thank him and recommit their business to the firm—while he uses the Call Path and appropriate communications practices—he should be well rewarded. He's doing what he has been trained to do, and he's getting the intended results.

If Bob, who sits across from Bill in the next cubicle, neither does the Call Path nor does he evoke the desired customer results, then his pay should be lower. He's not doing what he has been trained to do, and he's not getting the results that are expected of someone in his position.

If Bill and Bob received exactly the same amount of pay, this would be unfair. Moreover, it would undermine those reps who try to follow the rules and optimize customer outcomes and company results.

My clients, who have been thoroughly briefed in the systems outlined in this book, generally assign a 25–50% merit-pay component to the performance of reps on TEAMeasures. This is to say that all reps receive a basic salary that pays them an equal amount. But the remainder of their pay varies, based on their individual effectiveness.

I should say that, with SEAmeasures, managers are usually compensated in the same way. Part of their income is pre-established, but a significant component is received as merit pay. As the result of rewarding the entire team in this manner, everyone works toward the same objectives.

Merit pay systems are highly motivating, especially for people who are real contributors. These people realize that their effectiveness is recognized and valued. And other reps have a clear and realistic chance to improve their standards of living, as well. So, this system breeds respect as well as hope.

This system also avoids a common de-motivator. When the best reps see that the worst reps receive the same pay as they do, as happens in too many companies, they naturally resent this fact. Such forced egalitarianism sours the high achievers on their jobs and makes the company look foolish and poorly directed. By using merit pay, we avoid such a destructive situation.

SECRETS TO RETAINING THE BEST EMPLOYEES

Recently, I conducted a national seminar tour on the topic of eliminating turnover among employees who do intensive phone work, including service personnel. Before doing the programs, I personally conducted a phone survey of managers to discover what the best practices are with respect to retaining quality personnel.

Companies that retain good people, while virtually eliminating rep turnover, do these important things:

- They pay their people at a rate that exceeds industry averages. In many cases, the differences are substantial.

- They provide an array of benefits. These include a health care package that includes medical, dental, and eye care. One of the most significant benefits, from the standpoint of retaining employees, is a 401K or similar retirement plan.

- They tend to be in the vanguard of adopting family-friendly and community-conscious perks. These include flextime, job-sharing, van pools, and paid time off for volunteer work.

These findings call for some discussion.

The Advantages and Disadvantages of Raising Compensation Levels

You would think that providing above-average compensation for first-rate people only makes sense. But it's amazing to see what lengths companies will go to in order to avoid increasing the payroll. A dramatic example is a big-city newspaper that experiences a 400% or higher turnover rate in its circulation division. With 300 people on the phones, the paper has to go through 1,200 people every year just to keep the phones active. At an estimated cost of $5,000 to recruit, train, and lose a person after 90 days, the company loses about $6 million per year due to turnover. By simply redirecting the money it wastes on dealing with turnover, the company could nearly *double* the pay of existing reps! But it wouldn't have to offer such a huge jump in pay to have a major impact. It could raise compensation by only 25% and decimate its turnover rate—overnight.

Why wouldn't this media giant follow common sense and simply raise its wages? For one thing, it is part of a public company, so it would have to explain to securities analysts why its payroll costs jumped. Of course, it would be saving money in other areas by reducing turnover, but these reductions wouldn't be nearly as visible to outside evaluators and to shareholders. Additionally, there are political issues inside the company that would need to be addressed before a massive raise in pay could be instituted. What would other departments say if customer service received a significant increase, while the department next door obtained only a minor one?

Instead, the paper is more likely to decide to outsource the circulation function, because by doing so it would be cutting the employee head count, which would be responded to favorably by Wall Street. Yet, the actual per-hour cost to the newspaper of outsourcing could be significantly more than for keeping the unit in house. Nonetheless, higher pay will retain quality people. As I see it, we're going to pay, one way or another. So, why not do it directly by increasing the value of our people's pay envelopes?

Benefits

A recent radio report stated that a large percentage of the adult population in the United States isn't covered by a private health care plan. This is shocking in our day and age. Thus, it doesn't come as a surprise that firms that suffer the highest employee turnover rate are also least likely to provide a good health care package. The firms that have licked the turnover problem are most likely to provide benefits that include paid dental and eye care. They also provide 401K retirement plans, or other forms of profit sharing or stock options in order to attract and retain quality people. You might say that these firms envision keeping their people around, healthy and happy for some time to come, and that employees recognize this commitment in the benefits they're provided.

Family-Friendly and Community-Conscious Perks

A few years ago, it was fairly common for highly achieving people to face up to making a major career decision. In short, it was either have a family or have a fast-track job. In most corporations you just couldn't be on the "mommy or daddy track" and still be thought of as a serious member of the team.

Fortunately, this thinking is changing. Companies are appreciating that tomorrow's employees are today's children, and if they're neglected or poorly reared, there will be a huge price to pay. So, more and more firms are offering family-friendly working plans.

These plans include flextime and job sharing. Flextime enables people to choose their working hours, to some extent. For example, a working parent may want to start at 7 a.m. and be done by 3 in order to spend time with his or her growing family. Or, someone might choose to work ten hours a day, four days a week, in order to have three-day weekends.

Job sharing splits one full-time position between two workers. Each works half-time, either mornings or afternoons. Or, each person can work two and one-half days per week.

Some firms are also experimenting with telecommuting, which is also a plus for folks who need to keep an eye on infants. All of these practices tend to endear employer to employee and make a good job hard to leave.

Time off for volunteer activities is something that enlightened companies are increasingly providing, in addition to environmentally positive practices such as employee van pooling. How do these practices reduce turnover while increasing employee loyalty?

People enjoy being associated with companies that have a deserved reputation for being in the vanguard of change. Each of the provisions that we've discussed sends a message to employees that says, "We care, and we understand."

REWARDING CAREER PATHS

Nobody wants to feel stuck in a dead-end job. The great therapist Bruno Bettle-heim said that there is one thing that people can't live without—and that is hope. Few things will keep good people aboard like the justified hope that they have a bright future with an organization.

What kind of ladder should a great CSR expect to climb? In a service center with approximately 20 people, this is the typical career path:

Entry-level CSR

Senior CSR

Team Leader

Supervisor

Manager

In a rapidly growing firm, this can be a perfectly acceptable career path. In such an environment, there will always be a need for team leaders, supervisors, and, possibly, multiple managers. But in a more static situation, or in a small service unit, there will be fewer opportunities beyond Senior CSR or Team Leader, and this will represent a ceiling that will frustrate excellent people.

To avoid losing these folks to another firm that might offer them a promotion as well as a raise in pay, I suggest you consider using customer service as an initial "proving ground" for your company's future salespeople and marketers. A major client of mine has done this with great success. A member of the financial community, this company developed an objective to significantly cut its turnover rate. I suggested we use the customer service group as a pool from which to draw sales and marketing trainees.

My logic was fairly straightforward. The firm had invested many months in getting CSRs up to speed and licensed by the Securities and Exchange Commission. Reps were already "sold on" the company, and for those who had implemented the Call Path, it wasn't much of a stretch for them to learn new sales techniques.

By placing these high achievers in a sales or marketing unit, the firm could also easily justify giving them raises in pay, as well as commissions and bonuses. Everyone was happy. Reps had new, more lucrative and challenging career paths, while the company retained and motivated many of its best people.

Of course, selling and marketing are only two places where experienced CSRs and managers can make a contribution. They should be able to move into many other staff positions as well. It would be a natural fit for team leaders, supervisors, and managers to find a place in training or in human resources. For that matter, they should be welcome anywhere that people skills are valued.

This chapter has shown how to recruit, motivate, and retain quality CSRs. In our next and final chapter, we'll turn to the important topic of making a "corporate commitment" to excellence in service.

Making a Corporate Commitment to First-Class Customer Service

When I visited a Lenscrafters store to order a pair of reading glasses, a gentleman strode right up to me with a great, big smile and welcomed me. I looked at his name tag, which said that he was their "Greeter." His job is to make customers feel good about walking through their door. I must say, he did his job very well. This small gesture makes a positive and lasting impression.

Smart companies, like Lenscrafters, try to make a corporate-wide commitment to delivering first-class customer service. They invest substantial resources in training everyone who interacts with internal or with external customers—that is, on site or on the phone. They realize that it's insufficient to assign only one department the overarching task of keeping customers happy and on board. The best companies actively spread the gospel of communications effectiveness. In doing so, they treat all employees as if they're certified members of the Customer Service Department.

I'm going to discuss how commitments to service are made. Then I'll show you how to apply the principles and practices that you've read about in the previous chapters. Finally, I'll discuss what the "standard of care" can be for our associates who work outside formal customer service departments. These folks, who are employed in administration, credit and collections, technical support, sales, and telemarketing, can do a number of things to incorporate positive service values and techniques into their everyday routines.

Unfortunately, these employees tend to be the last ones to be trained in service skills, yet they need and benefit from the instruction just as much as anyone else. Furthermore, by helping them to improve, we can make sure that the entire company sparkles, and we can feel confident whenever we hand off a call to them, or when we contact them because a customer needs a team solution to their problem.

WHAT IS A CORPORATE COMMITMENT, ANYWAY?

There are several elements to making a corporate commitment that I'd like to clarify.

1. Commitments are more than framed slogans. Walk into many of America's shopping malls, and you'll find a store called Successories that sells nicely framed pictures and posters that bear inscriptions such as "The Customer Is Number One" and "If We Don't Serve Our Customers Someone Else Will." These are pleasant reminders of a corporate purpose, but they aren't a substitute for embedding excellent service techniques into our everyday routines. As linguists are fond of pointing out, "The map isn't the territory." Likewise, slogans and posters don't make great service outcomes happen. People do.

2. Commitment starts at the top but has to extend to all levels of personnel. I have been able to develop and refine the techniques explained in this book because senior managers in various companies were convinced that superior customer service is a lasting strategic advantage. They appreciate that outstanding service is something that can't be periodically legislated and then be abandoned. It needs to be consistently integrated into all our activities.

The measure of a manager's commitment can be seen in his or her willingness to risk both corporate capital and personal "career capital" to support initiatives that will culminate in service-related breakthroughs. Managers need to put themselves on the line and say that, come what may, they're going to invest heavily in creating and then maintaining customer relationships.

In practice, what does this mean?

Case in Point: Before getting the green light to start an extensive consulting project in a large service center, I met with a Senior VP of Customer Service, the President, and the CEO. During our conversation, I theorized that we could develop techniques to make customer transactions shorter, but better. Because the President and the VP were schooled in the idea that the amount of time we spend with customers is positively correlated with high customer satisfaction, they were reluctant to support investing in my hunch.

The CEO agreed with me and bought my analysis, although it was counterintuitive. It took a large amount of faith as well as courage for him to support a new idea from an outsider while overriding the opinions of his very sharp and highly compensated colleagues. But he did just that, and we were able to validate my assumptions and implement strategies that cut costs dramatically and enabled the firm to leapfrog ahead of its competitors in industry satisfaction surveys.

This is what I mean by "risking career capital." If my project hadn't worked out, the CEO wouldn't have been fired. But his image would have been tarnished at least a little, and he would have been slightly more reluctant in the future to assert his opinions in similar situations.

By the same token, numerous customer service managers and others who are far from the boardroom have attended seminars with me and have urged their companies to bring me in to consult. They've taken even greater career risks, relatively speaking, but they've also helped to reshape their service outcomes as a result.

3. Commitment to quality service must be continuously "sold" and its value continuously proven. *Sustained excellence in customer service won't happen unless your company's employees are continuously and completely sold on its value to them.*

How can we sell senior managers on the value of customer service? For them, service needs to be linked strongly to dollars and cents before the most powerful managers will completely hop on board with you and accept its value. Often they're paid based on how much they save or make for the company. Generally, they're not going to open the corporate coffers to support training and development to simply spread the gospel of service, unless they feel the messianic fervor themselves. Fundamentally, they care about profit, and they're paid to use all reasonable means to maximize it.

How does service raise profits? It keeps customers coming back, but how do we know this is true? Yes, we can point to our own anecdotal experiences that demonstrate to us that when we're treated well we tend to keep doing business with the better caregivers. But this is subjective proof, and it's not weighty enough to impress the hardest-bitten chief financial officers.

What they want is a link that demonstrates the *specific value* of a given service action and the repeat business it created. In other words, how can we prove that our great rep caused the customer to stay with us and to buy again?

This seems like an insurmountable obstacle, but please take a moment to review what we've covered in this book. If you use the Call Path and TEAMeasures or similar instruments, you can link your service behavior to a customer's future purchasing behavior.

There are at least a few ways to do this.

a. You can measure the Customer's Response during or after a specific transaction to determine if she recommitted—that is, if she verbally pledged loyalty to your company. If the answer is yes, then we have established that there is a stated intention or a promise to do additional business, induced by the good feelings generated during the transaction. Generally, people act in a manner consistent with their stated intentions and promises.

b. You can track this conversation into the future. Does this customer actually buy again within a certain period of time? If so, there is a connection between the stated promise to buy and the fulfillment of that specific promise. Likewise, it may be possible to assess a rep's performance by tracking a large number of the customers he or she has interacted with, to see what their subsequent purchasing behavior is like.

c. I have referred a number of times to my clients in the mutual fund industry. One of my clients validated TEAMeasures and the Call Path in three different ways. One was through an independent, mailed survey done by a consulting firm other than my own. They compared the customer service ratings of my client to other financial companies. My client emerged in the top 10%.

The second tool was a survey of brokers and customers that is regularly done by a well-known mutual fund advisory group. It ranked 26 mutual funds. Immediately before installing my program, my client was ranked 24th.

After our project, it leaped to 4th, and then it reached #1 and stayed there, five years in a row.

The third and perhaps most compelling validation was the company's own report of its assets under management before and after instituting my program. This is a clear measure of customer satisfaction and loyalty. If you maintain or grow assets you're in good shape, but if there is a "leeching" of assets, you're in trouble because customers are leaving the fold. I was informed that before my program there was a leeching of assets, and afterward, it stopped. While I wouldn't claim to be the exclusive agent of change, there were no significant other events or procedures put into place that could have accounted for the dramatic turnaround. Therefore, the inference was made that when we got customers to pledge their loyalty, it paid off.

All these outcomes contributed to confirming for senior managers that the ramped-up customer service efforts were worth the investment. Further, CSRs, team leaders, and supervisors became sold on the connection between what they were doing so well and the positive effects their performances were having on the company's reputation and bottom line. They could understand that by eliciting recommitments from customers they were in charge of maintaining customer loyalty. That's both empowering and motivating.

But we can do even more than this to encourage adoption and perpetuation of the best service techniques and routines.

4. Commitments to providing first-class service must be clearly, fairly and consistently compensated. We have to put our money where our mouths are if we hope to create a service culture in our organizations. Earlier I mentioned that managers will get more of those behaviors that they reward. If we reward excellence in service, we'll get more of it. Customer service people should earn merit pay, as should others who perform customer service without having this term in their job titles.

HELPING SPECIFIC DEPARTMENTS TO BECOME MORE EFFECTIVE COMMUNICATORS

Credit and Collections

I began my telephone career at the age of 18. I was a full-time collector for a finance company. My job was to remind people that their payments were overdue and to get them to commit to getting current by a certain "promise-to-pay" date. My effectiveness was measured a few ways. One was based on the number of calls I made. Another was determined by how much money I collected. In those days, the telephone communication standards were quite low, I must admit. My boss didn't care how brusque his people were, as long as they got debtors to pay their bills.

Today, this seems like a primitive way to approach the collections task. The trick to being effective as a collector is to get debtors to want to pay your bill first and to retain as much of their goodwill as we can.

This isn't easy, considering the fact that the collections call can be inherently offensive. Debtors can feel defensive, that their lateness in making payments is being criticized, while collectors can feel that debtors are really trying to avoid making their payments.

The key to producing a positive collections experience is to be found in a variant of the Call Path that I've produced for Customer Service. The goal of this outbound call is to elicit a promise to pay, but you'll probably notice that we also try to use supportive language throughout the conversation:

Collections Call Path: Outbound

Hello, ___? This is ___ ___ with ___ ___ on a recorded line. How are things with you, today? That's good.

I'm calling because I have an unpaid invoice dated _____, and I wanted to help you to get this taken care of. When has it been scheduled for payment, _____?

Okay, _____, then we should expect to get the payment by _____, is that right? We really appreciate it, and is there anything else I can help you with?

Well, thank you for doing business with us!

(Did you know we also accept major credit cards? Why don't we just take care of it that way, okay?)

What language jumps out at you as being especially supportive? How about this phrase:

And I wanted to help you to get this taken care of . . .

I have to admit that I'm proud of this one, because it's so untraditional in a collections call. Psychologically, it's in keeping with the Promise of Help that we've inserted into customer service calls. It tells the debtor that we're on his side and that we're actually trying to help him bring his account up to date. This is dramatically different from the adversarial, us-against-them messages that most collectors use.

We also offer Additional Help as well as use a Recommitment line. Why, you might ask, do we try to recommit customers who are late in paying their bills? Almost every individual or organization experiences cash-flow problems at some time, but they can also recover from such woes. So, why alienate them when we can make them feel good about doing business with all divisions of our firm, including the credit or collections department?

I'm reminded of a story that I heard about the Billy Graham ministry. It came to the attention of Mr. Graham that a fellow was facing dire financial circumstances in his printing business. He wasn't a churchgoer, nor was he even a member of Mr. Graham's denomination. A representative phoned the troubled fellow and offered him the opportunity to print Mr. Graham's flyers. This action literally saved his business and helped to turn his life around. By showing faith and confidence in the printer, the Graham Ministry created a friend and supporter for life, while doing a lot of good for someone in need. That's what we do when we treat debtors with respect and when we try to help them to help themselves out of their payment difficulties. When they get on their feet, they'll remember us for our exceptional treatment of them. This is just another way to deliver great service throughout our organizations.

Let's Train the Shipping Department, Too

CSRs are often challenged by agitated customers: "Where's my shipment? It hasn't arrived yet!" Often, reps can check the order status in their computers, but if that doesn't help them to find the problem, they need to call their shipping department.

Sadly, many of the people who rise through the ranks in operations-related departments, such as in shipping, haven't had much of a chance to polish their communications skills. In fact, they can be somewhat abrasive because they haven't been trained in people skills. They present a golden opportunity to spread the gospel of company-wide excellence in service. Shippers can be called on to smoothly interact with their associates, who will then pass along their good feelings to customers.

Technical Support Can Offer More Than Technical Solutions

Technical support reps also deserve to receive customer service skills training. After all, they interact with customers on a daily basis, and their communication techniques will influence customers' loyalty to our firms.

When we know a great deal about a topic, as "techies" do, it's easy to fall into the trap of sounding pompous. In the long run, the arrogant among us are almost always humbled by competitors who offer better service, or even newer technologies. Instead of standing by us in times of difficulty or transition, clients flee because there is so little goodwill bonding them to offensive technicians and their companies.

I've actually heard technical support reps say that, if they sound "too nice," customers will think they're "airheads." Where is it written that people can't sound both smart and nice? More than one management guru has said, quite rightly, that we should invest in our relationships with clients, because, in the long run, they're the only potentially permanent, competitive advantage.

We're All Becoming Salespeople

Until the 1990s, companies were filled with specialists who focused on handling very narrow jobs. And then the 90s ushered in a different mind-set. Companies started deploying interdisciplinary teams to tackle problems and to exploit opportunities. No longer could someone hide behind an excuse such as, "Customer service isn't a part of my position description, so I don't have to do it!"

Everybody, these days, is responsible for keeping customers happy. Customer service personnel are being asked to stretch their skills beyond simply answering questions and smoothing ruffled feathers. *Increasingly, CSRs are being asked to sell as an integral part of doing their jobs.*

As a consultant, I'm called on to help CSRs and their managers adjust their attitudes and their skills so they can transform Customer Service from being a cost center into becoming a profit center, as well. I see this as a growing trend, and it can mean several positive things for people who receive cross training in sales skills:

1. CSRs, as well as managers, can ask for and justify raises in pay.
2. More jobs can open up for CSRs who sell well. They can become trainers, supervisors, telesales people, and field salespeople, if they wish.

3. Based on their contributions to profits, successful salespeople can enjoy greater visibility and recognition within their companies.

4. Reps and managers who learn selling strategies will also become attractive to headhunters and to other firms that will pay well for people possessing sales and sales management skills.

Transforming CSRs into "Universal Agents"

Universal agents are individuals who have been trained in both service and selling skills. Theoretically, they can perform service functions when inbound call volumes are high, say on Mondays, Tuesdays, and Wednesdays. But, on Thursdays and Fridays, when they are no longer needed on the service desk, they can switch to making outbound telemarketing calls.

Service Should Be Proactive

Try calling your clients two or three times a year, simply to say hello. Here are just a few of the benefits you can realize:

1. You can find out how they're using your products or services. I call past participants in my public seminars and ask them how they're using the information they learned. I discover what was most useful to them, over the long term. This enables me to adjust my course content to emphasize the more valued lessons.

2. By staying in touch, we can discover their unmet needs. If I have a product that can fulfill those needs, I'm able to make another sale. For example, a number of seminar attendees wanted a little more help with implementing my ideas, but they didn't need consulting. So, I recommended my audio seminars, which ended up being a perfect fit.

3. You can update your files. Any list of business people becomes 10–20% obsolete each year. People change jobs, and companies merge and move.

4. You can get valuable feedback about your products and services. I thought one manager was less than elated with one of our seminars, so I called her. I discovered that she actually appreciated the program. Two months later, when I scheduled another seminar, she sent four of her associates over a thousand miles to attend it!

5. You can earn testimonials. This is an extremely important, yet uncultivated area, for most service people. It's always valuable to have a positive reference at the ready for a new prospect to call or refer to.

Case in Point: For instance, last year I was called by someone in the concrete business who had read one of my books. We got to talking about my audio programs, and he expressed interest in buying one, but he doubted if he could get approval from his boss. "How persuasive would it be if your boss saw a positive letter about me from the Prestressed Concrete Institute?" I asked. I faxed it over, and within 24 hours my prospect obtained the necessary approval.

In another case, I called someone whom I had trained at Xerox ten years before. He had moved on to build a great career in the securities industry. I asked him how my training compared to other sources. He said, "Altogether, I've had about nine months of sales training, when you add it all up, and by far, yours was the best!" He said I could quote him, and I have, with positive effect.

6. You can earn referrals. People know other people who can buy. Do what insurance salespeople have been doing for nearly a century—ask for referrals. But to earn the right to a referral, you should stay in touch with your customers over the long term. Call your client base two or three times a year, and you'll see what I mean.

The Best Service Tip of All: Do Something Extra All the Time!

One of the best ways to win the gratitude and loyalty of any customer is by doing something special that competitors aren't doing. It's a way of standing out, and it is especially helpful if you sell a product or service that is otherwise indistinguishable from your competition's.

Case in Point: There is an Italian restaurant in Los Angeles called Palermo that does this in a creative fashion. It has limited seating, so it often takes up to an hour to get a table. How could it make customers feel better about waiting?

It answered this question by giving away free wine or soft drinks to customers in the waiting area. By doing this, Palermo developed a loyal, though slightly marinated, customer base. This small gesture enabled them to outgrow their first location, so the owners found a much bigger site. When they opened the larger restaurant, waiting times were cut to 15–20 minutes, but they continued to dispense free drinks. It became a tradition, as well as a symbol of friendship and generosity.

In all likelihood, you're not in the restaurant business, so what can you do? Have all employees who work at your company ask this question of themselves. How can they improve their service? What special services can they bestow on internal and external customers? When everyone can answer these questions, you'll know you have made a corporate commitment to delivering first-class customer service.

AFTERWORD

Thank you for reading this book. I hope you got a lot out of it. If you have any questions, or if you need assistance in applying these new principles or procedures, please contact me. We offer consulting and a complete line of speeches, seminars, and training products that may be of assistance.

In the meantime, good luck!

Dr. Gary S. Goodman
The Goodman Organization, Inc.
631 W. Broadway
Glendale, CA 91204
Voice: (818) 243–7338
Fax: (818) 956–2242
E-mail: goodmanorg@earthlink.net

INDEX

CocaCola, 57

Communication: in coaching and counseling sessions, 113⁻117; direct pointing technique in, 64; nonverbal, 113⁻114; open, and workroom environment, 126⁻127. *See also* Conversational structure

Company information, representativeís delivery of, 127

Compensation: increases, advantages and disadvantages of, 142⁻143; pay-for-performance, 140⁻142

Competitive advantage, 11

Conflict prevention, 42⁻43

Conversational structure: appropriateness/relevance measure for, 37⁻38; calibration in, 33⁻34; length, as performance indice, 75⁻76; P.E.P. formula for, 38⁻40; transitional phrasing in, 40⁻41. See also Pitch patterns; Speech patterns

Courtesy, 29⁻30

Credit and collections, 151⁻153

Criticism: constructive, acceptance of, 132; high grade, 115⁻116. *See also* Feedback

Customer: appreciation, 3–4, 6; blaming of, 5; difficult, defusing conflict with, 41–45; loyalty, great service encounter and, 10; regaining trust of, 8; repeat, 5, 10

Customer recommitment, service routine and, 22–23

Customer satisfaction, distinctive signs of, 14

Customer service: personality-driven versus process-driven, 9–10; proactive, 155–156; superior, basic characteristics of, 5–11. *See also* Service monitoring; Service quality

Customer service representative (CSR): as crisis manager, 41–45; ideal, attributes of, 27–30, 35–47, 130–135; listening skills of, 45–46; personality profiling and, 93–94. *See also* Pitch patterns; Speech patterns

Customer surveys, 55–57

Customer testimonials, uses of, 52–55, 156

D

Defensive messages, avoidance of, 43–45

Dress codes, 63–64

Drucker, P. F., 9

Management: controlling attitudes versus behaviors in, 59; criticism balanced with praise in, 60; essential practices of, 112–128; and participative decision making (PDM), 113; role modeling, 125–126; training, in counseling and coaching, 119–120. *See also* SEAmeasures (Supervisor Effectiveness Assessment)

Managing by walking around (MBWA), 58–61, 124–125

Measurement systems, criteria in, 76–77. See also Telephone Effectiveness Assessment Measures (TEAMeasures)

Merit pay, 140–142, 151

Monitoring. *See* Service monitoring

Mood swings, contaminating effects of, 58, 62

Morale, monitoring and, 50–51

Motivation: levels of, 72–73; merit pay and, 140–142

Musicians, as customer service representatives, 133

N

Negative publicity, guarantees and, 7

New business promotion, guarantees and, 7

O

Objective-setting process, articulation of, 116–117

Offer of additional help: evaluation of, 85; proper tone for, 21

P

Participative decision making (PDM), 113

P.E.P. (Point Evidence Point) Formula, 38–40

Performance evaluations, 75–106; based on number and length of transactions, 75–76; identification of scorable events in, 121–122; monitoring and, 50. *See also* Telephone Effectiveness Assessment Measures (TeaMeasures)

Performance standards, objective-setting process and, 116–117

Personal responsibility, supervisorís promotion of, 117–118

Pitch patterns: calibrated to text, 18–21, 23

Promise of help: evaluation and, 83; proper tone for, 20–21

Psychological profiling, avoidance of, 93–94

Q

Quality service: communication factors in, 27–46; corporate commitment to, 148–151; and customer satisfaction, signals of, 14

R

Referrals, 156

Repeat business, promotion of, 5, 10

S

Sale transaction, 8, 154–155

Satisfaction guarantees: and firmís quality orientation, 9; need for, 6–8; servicing of, 8

Scorable events, identification of, 87–92, 121–122

SEAmeasures (Supervisor Effectiveness Assessment), 108–128; coaching sessions and, 112–124; instrument, 109–111; and managing by walking around, 124–125; supervisor evaluation in, 110; supervisor training in, 119–120

Self-scoring strategy, motivation and, 118–119

Service monitoring, 49–73; and managing by walking around (MBWA), 58–61; rationale, 49–51; superficial approach (monitoring-by-exception), 52–55; through surveys and questionnaires, 55–57. *See also* Call recording

Service quality: communication factors in, 27–46; corporate commitment to, 148–151

Service routine. *See* Universal Call Path

Shipping department, 153

Speech patterns: articulation of words in, 30–31; assessment measures of, 87–92; calibration in, 33–34; evaluation of, 100–102; give-and-take sequence in, 33–34; pitch patterns in, 18–21, 23, 32–33; variable volume in, 33; vocabulary and grammar in, 34–35; vocal intensity in, 33; vocal rate in, 31–32

Starbucks, 41

Supervisor evaluation. *See* SEAmeasures (Supervisor Effectiveness Assessment)

T

Taping of calls. *See* Call recording

Technical support staff, 154

Team leaders. *See* Management; SEAmeasures

TEAMeasures (Telephone Effectiveness Assessment Measures), 77–106; call interpretation guidelines in, 87–91; caveats and drawbacks, 93–94, 100; coaching and counseling session, 81–86; definitions of scorable events in, 87–92; as prescriptive tool, 77–78, 95; as recruiting tool, 100–105; scoring system, 78, 79–86, 94–100, 103; stop-loss provision in, 83; usefulness of, 105–106

Telephone sales, 154–155; and guarantees, 8

Time/Life, 63

Tonal patterns, *See* Pitch patterns

U

Universal Call Path, 11–26, 65; artistry in, 12; call conclusion in, 17; coaching/counseling session, 117; customer recommitment and, 22–23; measuring compliance with, 81–86, 87; motivation for using, 72–73; offer of additional help in, 17–18, 21; positive results of, 11; promise of help in, 16–17, 20, 24; supervisor training in, 119–120; troubleshooting, 24–26; unscripted portion of, 24–25; variant of, 152–153; and vocal (pitch) pattern, 18–21, 23

V

Vocabulary, 34–35

Vocal pattern, 18–21, 23

Vocal rates, 31–32

W

Warranties, 8

Work environment: codes of conduct and dress in, 62, 63–64; individual moods and attitudes in, 58–59, 62; morale in, 50–51; open communication in, 126–127

Printed in the United Kingdom
by Lightning Source UK Ltd.
126275UK00001B/47-52/A

9 780787 951399